A
LEBANESE
Harvest

A
LEBANESE
Harvest

Traditional Vegetarian Recipes

Nouhad Boulos-Guillaume

GARNET PUBLISHING

A Lebanese Harvest
Traditional Vegetarian Recipes

Copyright © 1993 English language edition Garnet Publishing Limited
© Edifra/Ediframo, Paris

Published by
Garnet Publishing Limited
8 Southern Court
South Street,
Reading RG1 4QS
UK

First edition 1993
Reprinted 1998

ISBN 1 873938 04 7

British Library Cataloguing in Publication Data
A catalogue record for this book is available from the British Library

Illustrations: Anne Lester
Project management and layouts: Jackie Jones
Design: Christine Wood
Translation: Heather Jones, Rima Fawaz al Husseine
Reprographics: MacImage, London

Printed in Lebanon

CONTENTS

INTRODUCTION

Lebanese cuisine has become renowned amongst culinary experts and food connoisseurs the world over for its wide variety of well balanced, healthy and appetizing food. There have been many books written on the subject, but these have concentrated upon the meat-based recipes, and have overlooked an important side of Lebanese cuisine, which is commonly known as bil zeit (cooking 'in oil')

This book offers the reader a wide variety of recipes cooked 'in oil', an expression which traditionally refers to a diet free of meat, chicken or fish. These recipes draw on a wide variety of ingredients - grains, pulses, fresh vegetables, eggs and yogurt - all flavoured and seasoned with various aromatic herbs. They form a very nutritious, healthy diet.

There are basically two kinds of recipe in this book. First, there are dishes which are known to all Lebanese, regardless of region and eating habits, such as chickpeas with tahini (hummos), or tabbouleh. Secondly, there is a wide variety of regional dishes most common to the north of the country, some of which have almost forgotten, such as potato kibbeh, potato mhar'sa or amhiyyeh with yogurt.

HOW TO SERVE THESE RECIPES

The recipes in this book are not for traditional three-course meals. They have been compiled with the aim of providing a wide range of attractive and appetising dishes which can be served as hors d'oeuvre (hot or cold) or any mixed spread, and which are especially suitable for entertaining.

INGREDIENTS: WHAT YOU SHOULD KNOW

- Freshness is all important. Avoid using frozen or canned vegetables, as they lose both flavour and vitamins in the processing

- When buying greens, look for fresh, bright colours - avoid yellowed leaves, blackened stems and any vegetables that are limp or faded.

- Wash dried beans or lentils well to remove dust and, possibly, stones.

- Always soak dried beans before cooking, preferably overnight.

- Keep your store cupboards well stocked with a wide range of spices and seasonings. Their use can alter the whole character of a dish. Use exactly as recommended in the recipes.

- Most of the ingredients should be readily available, through health-food stores, good supermarkets or oriental stores.

- Do not exceed the measures indicated in each recipe.

EQUIPMENT AND COOKING METHODS

Traditionally, pots and pans were made out of clay and copper, and the cooking process was slow, taking place on a wood-fired cooking range. In order to adapt traditional recipes to the present-day kitchen, I have chosen a two-step method for those ingredients which require long cooking: beans, chickpeas, and other grains are first boiled in a pressure-cooker, then the cooking process completed in a heavy-bottomed saucepan. Using this method will save you time, quality and flavour.

MEASUREMENTS

The measuring utensils used are: a cup, a tablespoon and a teaspoon.

N.B. Some recipes have illustrations that show a spoon - this means that the dish should remain liquid in consistency.

Bon appetit!

Nouhad Boulos-Guillaume

CHAPTER 1

BASIC RECIPES AND TECHNIQUES

PREPARING AND COOKING RICE

TWO KINDS OF RICE ARE USED IN
THESE RECIPES: LONG GRAIN AND
SHORT GRAIN. EACH RECIPE SPECIFIES
WHICH KIND IS TO BE USED. PRE-
COOKED RICE IS NOT RECOMMENDED.
REMEMBER TO USE THE SAME SIZE CUP
TO MEASURE BOTH THE RICE AND THE
WATER.

Pour the rice into a large saucepan. Add cold water, stir lightly and cover. The quantities used should be exactly as indicated in the recipe.

Begin cooking rice over a high heat, reduce to moderate and finish cooking over a low heat. The cooking time will be indicated in the recipe.

Remove rice from the heat, stir once more and leave to swell.

N.B. Rice should always be cooked covered.

PREPARING BULGUR WHEAT

BULGUR WHEAT, BURGHUL OR BURGUL,
IS A WHOLE WHEAT WHICH HAS BEEN
PARTIALLY COOKED AND IS USUALLY
CRACKED. IT COMES IN THREE GRADES:
COARSE, MEDIUM AND FINE. RED
BULGUR WHEAT IS PREFERABLE BUT IS
NOT EASILY FOUND. BULGUR WHEAT
SHOULD NOT BE CONFUSED WITH
COUSCOUS, WHICH IS SIMILAR, BUT
MORE REFINED AND USUALLY MORE
EXPENSIVE.

SOAKING METHOD

Place in a bowl the amount of bulgur wheat indicated in the recipe. Cover with cold water and stir gently so that all the grains are saturated. (You can use fingertips to separate the grains.)

Allow to stand for several minutes, allowing the grains to settle at the bottom of the bowl.

Drain off the excess water.

Leave to soak for whatever length of time is indicated in the recipe used.

COOKING METHOD

The method for cooking is generally the same in all the dishes cooked with bulgur wheat:

Cover the pot, bring to the boil over a high heat, reduce to a moderate heat and finish cooking over a low heat. The cooking time will be indicated in the recipe used.

Turn off the heat and leave bulgur wheat to swell in a covered pot for 3–5 minutes.

N.B. Bulgur wheat is soaked only if specified in the recipe; otherwise it is used as it is.

PREPARING A GARLIC SAUCE

IN THESE RECIPES GARLIC IS ALWAYS GROUND, UNLESS IT IS COOKED. TO OBTAIN THE BEST RESULTS, IT IS BEST TO GRIND THE GARLIC WITH A PESTLE AND MORTAR, PREFERABLY WOODEN.

Peel garlic, cut each clove into 2 or 3 sections and place in the mortar.

Add a good pinch of salt and grind until all pieces are completely crushed and no fibres remain.

Pour in a few drops of oil and mix with the pestle, stirring clockwise.

When all the oil has been absorbed by the garlic, pour in the same amount of oil again and mix once more. This process can be repeated until the mixture starts to resemble mayonnaise.

Once the ground garlic is saturated with oil, dilute with vinegar, lemon or lime juice as indicated in the recipe.

PREPARING AND COOKING CHICKPEAS

NOWADAYS, CHICKPEAS ARE VERY EASY TO PREPARE: JUST POUR PLENTY OF BOILING WATER OVER THEM AND SOAK FOR 2–3 HOURS, THEN RINSE AND COOK.

THE TRADITIONAL METHOD OF PREPARATION IS DESCRIBED BELOW—IT INCLUDES REMOVAL OF THE CHICKPEA SKIN AFTER COOKING. MANY PEOPLE NOW LEAVE THE SKINS INTACT, FOR THEIR NUTRITIONAL VALUE.

Pick over the chickpeas, if necessary, and soak in 5-6 times their volume of cold water.

Half a teaspoon of bicarbonate of soda can be added to accelerate the cooking and to make the chickpeas more digestible.

The next day spread the chickpeas out on a cloth and roll a rolling pin over them until the skins break and the grains split in two.

Pour chickpeas into a big bowl filled with water. The grains will settle at the bottom while the skins rise to the surface.

Remove the skins using a straining spoon, then drain the grains in a colander.

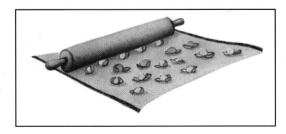

N.B. Chickpeas are then used as indicated in the recipe.

PREPARING TAHINI
(SESAME CREAM)

TAHINI, TAHINEH OR TAHINA (SESAME PASTE)
CAN BE FOUND IN DELICATESSEN SHOPS,
HEALTHFOOD SHOPS AND MANY SUPERMARKETS,
GENERALLY IN JARS OR SOMETIMES CANS. SESAME
PASTE IS VERY THICK AND DOES NOT MIX EASILY
WITH OTHER INGREDIENTS, THEREFORE WHEN IT
IS USED IN A RECIPE THE FOLLOWING
PRELIMINARY PREPARATION IS NECESSARY TO
TRANSFORM THE PASTE INTO A CREAM.

To soften the paste, gradually add a few drops of lemon or lime juice (as specified in recipe) and beat the mixture with a fork.

When the juice is first added, you will notice the paste harden. Continue beating, adding juice until the cream is the consistency of thick whipped cream. (If it remains too thick, add a few drops of water.)

Use tahini as indicated in the recipe.

COOKING PINE NUTS (PIGNOLIA)

PINE NUTS, OR PIGNOLIA, ARE THE
EDIBLE SEEDS OF PINE CONES. MANY
COUNTRIES PRODUCE THEM, BUT WE
RECOMMEND THE USE OF THOSE FROM
THE MEDITERRANEAN COUNTRIES.
THEY ARE AVAILABLE FROM MANY
OUTLETS, PARTICULARLY
DELICATESSENS AND HEALTH FOOD
STORES. THEIR USE IN LEBANESE
COOKING ENRICHES THE DISH AND
LENDS A DISTINCTIVE FLAVOUR.

Heat 2-3 tablespoonfuls of oil in a skillet (exact quantities are indicated in each recipe).

Add the pine nuts and stir constantly until they turn a golden colour.

Quickly remove from the skillet and spread them onto a plate.

Use as indicated in the recipe.

FRYING ONIONS: TWO METHODS

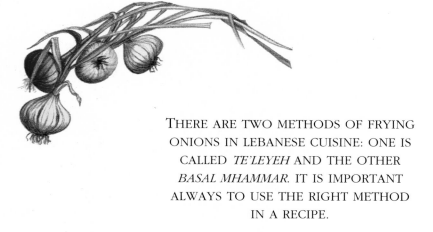

THERE ARE TWO METHODS OF FRYING ONIONS IN LEBANESE CUISINE: ONE IS CALLED *TE'LEYEH* AND THE OTHER *BASAL MHAMMAR*. IT IS IMPORTANT ALWAYS TO USE THE RIGHT METHOD IN A RECIPE.

THE BASAL MHAMMAR METHOD

Peel the onions and slice very finely, as shown.

Fry in oil, stirring constantly.

Remove from heat when they turn golden brown.

Use as indicated in the recipe.

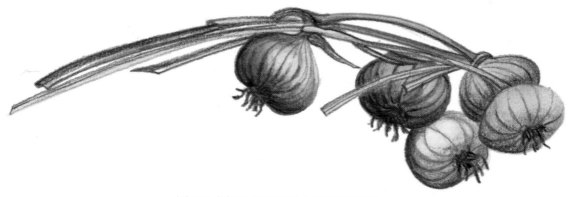

THE TE'LEYEH METHOD

Peel the onions and chop very finely, as shown.

Put the oil and chopped onions in a skillet and fry on a high heat for a few minutes, stirring frequently.

When the onions start to turn golden, reduce the heat. Keep stirring until the onions are golden brown (caramel colour) all over—be careful as onions burn easily at this stage.

Remove from heat and immediately add ¼ cup of water to halt the cooking process.

Use as indicated in the recipe.

CHAPTER 2

FRESH VEGETABLES

GREEN BEANS WITH GARLIC SAUCE

Lubyeh b-zeit w-tum

Preparation time: 35 minutes
Cooking time: 25 minutes
SERVES 4

1 kg (2lb) tender green beans

300 g (10oz) broad beans

1 potato

salt

FOR GARLIC SAUCE

4 cloves garlic

3 tbsp olive oil (use extra virgin cold pressed olive oil if possible)

juice of ½ lime

String the green beans if necessary; remove the outer shells of the broad beans.

Wash and boil the two types of bean separately.

Boil (or even better, steam) the potato.

Drain off the green beans and rinse the broad beans in cold water.

Lightly squeeze green beans with hands to extract excess water.

Mix the broad beans and the well drained green beans together.

Prepare a garlic sauce (see page 4) with the garlic, oil and lime juice.

Pour the sauce over the beans.

Add a pinch of salt, a few drops of olive oil, and mix.

Serve garnished with slices of steamed potato.

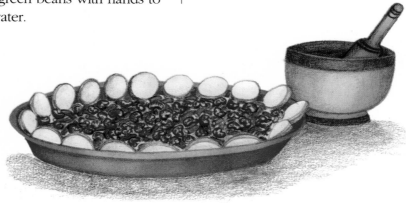

GREEN BEANS WITH CORIANDER

Lubyeh b-kozbra

Preparation time: 20 minutes
Cooking time: 40 minutes
SERVES 4

1 kg (2lb) extra fine green beans
6 tbsp olive oil
2 bunches coriander
3 cloves garlic
salt
1 tomato

String beans (if necessary) and cut lengthwise.

Wash and leave to drain in a colander.

Heat oil in a pan, add beans and stir for 10 minutes over a moderate heat.

When beans start to soften, add just sufficient water to cover them.

Cover the saucepan and bring to the boil.

Cook uncovered over a moderate heat until all the water has completely evaporated.

Wash the coriander and chop coarsely.

Grind the garlic. Add garlic and the coriander to the beans, continuing to cook over a high heat.

Salt to taste.

Stir for 3-4 minutes.

Serve garnished with tomato slices.

GREEN BEANS WITH SPRING ONIONS

Lubyeh m'elleyeh

> *Preparation time:* 30 minutes
> *Cooking time:* 45 minutes
> SERVES 4

1 kg (2lb) tender green beans

500 g (1lb) onions

½ cup oil

salt, black pepper

1 bunch spring onions

String green beans (if necessary) and cut in half.

Wash and leave to drain.

Slice the onions very thinly and brown in oil, using a saucepan or flameproof casserole.

When onions turn golden, add the beans and salt. Cook over a moderate heat for about 20 minutes, stirring every 3 minutes.

Half cover with water, cover the pan and cook over a moderate heat for a further 25 minutes.

Remove saucepan lid and bring to the boil to reduce the liquid.

Sprinkle with pepper, garnish with spring onions, and serve.

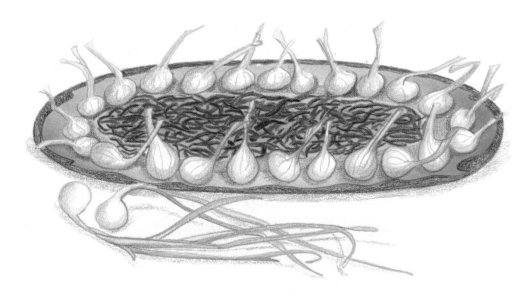

BROAD BEANS WITH TOMATOES
Lubyeh m'elleyeh b-banadura

Preparation time: 20 minutes
Cooking time: 45 minutes

1 kg (2lb) broad beans
1 medium onion
4 ripe tomatoes, peeled and seeds removed
3 tbsp vegetable oil
2 cloves garlic
1 potato
salt, black pepper
a small pinch cayenne
a pinch cumin
1 bunch radishes
1 bunch spring onions

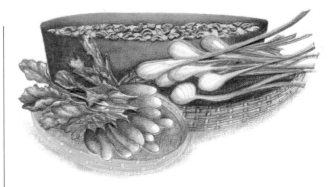

Shell the beans, wash, and drain well.

Coarsely chop the onion and fry in oil until golden.

Dice tomatoes, and add to the pan with the onions.

Soften tomatoes over moderate heat for 10 minutes.

Meanwhile slice the garlic very finely and peel and dice the potato.

Add garlic, potato, shelled broad beans, salt, cayenne and black pepper to the onion and tomato mixture.

Add sufficient water to cover vegetables by about 1 cm ($^1/_2$ inch).

Cover the pan and boil for 5 minutes.

Reduce to a moderate heat and cook for 15–20 minutes.

Season to taste and sprinkle with the cumin.

Serve with radishes and spring onions.

BRAISED CABBAGE WITH BULGUR WHEAT
Makmura

> *Preparation time:* 20 minutes
> *Cooking time:* 40 minutes
> SERVES 4

½ cup coarse bulgur wheat
1 small head of white cabbage
1 large onion
½ cup olive oil
salt, pepper

Soak bulgur wheat (see page 3).

Discard the wilted outer leaves of the cabbage, and wash the remainder. Discard large central stalks from the cabbage leaves and slice the leaves finely.

Slice the onion finely.

Heat the oil in a large heavy-bottomed saucepan and fry the onions until golden.

Add the cabbage and fry over a moderate heat for about ¼ hour, stirring frequently.

Ccover the pan and simmer over a low heat for a further 10 minutes.

Add the soaked bulgur wheat and cook for 10 minutes, stirring constantly.

Add salt and pepper and serve hot.

BRAISED MIXED VEGETABLES

Masbeht al-fu'ra

> *Preparation time:* 20 minutes
> *Cooking time:* 60 minutes
> SERVES 4

2 aubergines
2 courgettes
2 ripe tomatoes, peeled and seeds removed
1 onion, finely sliced
2 tbsp olive oil
2 cloves garlic, peeled and finely sliced
salt
black pepper

Wash and peel the aubergines and courgettes.

Cut both vegetables into slices about 2 cm (3/4 inch) thick.

Heat oil in a large heavy-bottomed saucepan and fry onions until golden brown.

Add aubergine and courgette slices to the pan.

Using a spatula, mix and stir-fry for a few minutes.

Dice tomatoes and add to the other vegetables. Cook over a low heat for 10 minutes, stirring frequently.

Add garlic.

Add 1 cup of salted water, cover, and simmer over a low heat for 40 minutes, then serve.

COURGETTES SEASONED WITH CINNAMON

Mnazlet kusa

Preparation time: 15 minutes
Cooking time: 45 minutes
SERVES 4

3 courgettes
medium onions, very finely sliced
3 tbsp olive oil
2 ripe tomatoes
salt, pepper
1 tsp cinnamon

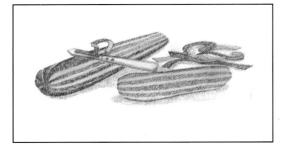

Wash the courgettes and peel as shown in illustration, removing only strips of the skin.

Cut into slices 2 cm (¾ inch) thick.

Heat oil in a large heavy-bottomed saucepan and fry onions until golden brown.

Add sliced courgette to the onions, cover pan and cook, stirring frequently, for 5–10 minutes.

Dice the tomatoes, and add to the vegetable mixture.

Add 2 cups of water and season with salt and pepper.

Cook covered over a moderate heat without stirring for half an hour.

Sprinkle with cinnamon and serve.

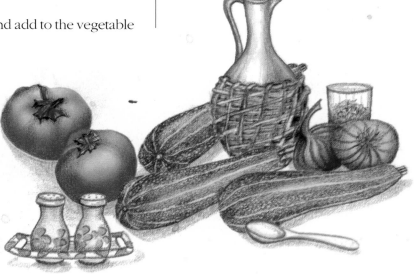

BRAISED AUBERGINES WITH CHICKPEAS

Mnazlet batinjan

Preparation time: 25 minutes
Cooking time: 1 hour
+ overnight soaking for chickpeas

½ cup dried chickpeas

2 aubergines

4 ripe tomatoes

2 medium onions

½ cup olive oil

4 cloves garlic

1 cup water

salt, pepper

Soak chickpeas overnight, and prepare (see page 5).

Prepare vegetables: Wash and peel aubergines. Cut into slices 1 cm (½ inch) thick. Wash tomatoes, peel, remove seeds, and dice. Peel onions and chop coarsely.

Fry the onions in the oil until golden brown.

Add tomatoes and prepared chickpeas and cook for 5-10 minutes.

Add peeled whole cloves of garlic, sliced aubergines, and 1 cup of water; season with salt and pepper.

Cover pan and cook over a high heat for 5 minutes.

Reduce heat and simmer for 40 minutes.

Remove garlic cloves and serve seasoned with a pinch of pepper.

SPINACH WITH ONIONS
Sbaneg m'alla

Preparation time: 20 minutes
Cooking time: 30 minutes
SERVES 4

1 kg (2lb) spinach

basal mhammar prepared with 3 onions

½ cup vegetable oil

FOR GARLIC SAUCE

2 small limes

¼ cup olive oil

3 cloves garlic

Wash spinach and remove the central leaf stalks, but do not throw them away. Slice the leaves.

Bring 2 litres (3½ pints) of salted water to the boil.

Add spinach leafstalks and boil for 5 minutes.

Add leaves and boil for a further 10-15 minutes.

Remove when stalks are soft and tender (use a fork to test).

Drain spinach leaves and squeeze between your hands until all excess moisture is removed.

Coarsely chop both the leaves and the ribs.

Prepare the basal mhammar with the oil and onions (see page 9).

Set aside half the fried onions on a plate.

Add the chopped spinach to the skillet with the rest of the onions.

Prepare a garlic sauce with the garlic, olive oil and lime juice (see page 4).

Pour sauce over spinach and mix well.

Serve garnished with the rest of the basal mhammar.

20

GREEN BEANS WITH BULGUR WHEAT
Madfunet lubyeh

Preparation time: 20 minutes
Cooking time: 45 minutes
SERVES 4

500 g (1lb) tender green beans
2 onions
4 tbsp olive oil
1 large cup coarse bulgur wheat
salt, pepper
1 bunch spring onions
1 bunch radishes

String the beans if necessary, remove stalks and wash

Cut into pieces 1 cm ($^1/_2$ inch) long.

Drain well.

Peel and slice onions finely.

Heat oil in a large heavy-bottomed saucepan and fry onions until golden brown.

Add beans, stir and cover. Simmer over a low heat for 20 minutes, stirring frequently.

When beans are cooked, add unsoaked bulgur wheat and 3$^1/_2$ cups of boiling water.

Add salt and pepper and simmer over a moderate heat for 10 minutes.

Reduce heat and cook for another 15 minutes.

Remove from heat and leave to swell for a few minutes.

Serve garnished with radishes and spring onions.

SALAD OF BULGUR WHEAT AND FINE HERBS
Tabbuleh

Preparation time: 1 hour
SERVES 4

½ cup fine bulgur wheat
3 tomatoes
1 small cucumber
1 small green pimento (optional)
4 bunches parsley
1 bunch chives
1 bunch fresh mint
1 sprig basil
1 small Spanish onion
juice of 3 lemons
1 cup extra virgin olive oil
1 tsp each: salt, black pepper, cinnamon, paprika
a pinch cayenne
1 cos lettuce

Chop the 4 kinds of herbs as finely as possible. The finer they are chopped, the better the flavour will be.

Dice the tomatoes, cucumber and pimento.

Finely chop the onions, add a pinch of salt, and gently rub in for a few seconds.

Mix together the soaked bulgur wheat with the tomatoes, cucumber, onion, pimento and herbs in a large bowl.

Add salt, black pepper, spices, oil and lemon juice.

Mix well and put in the refrigerator for 15 minutes.

Serve accompanied with lettuce.

Soak bulgur wheat for 15–25 minutes (see page 3).

Wash the tomatoes, cucumber, pimento and herbs, and drain thoroughly (if in hurry, dry with a cloth).

BRAISED VEGETABLES WITH FINE HERBS

Sli' m'alla

Preparation time: 30 minutes
Cooking time: 25 minutes
SERVES 4

½ cup coarse bulgur wheat

1 kg (2lb) fresh spinach

1 kg (2lb) fresh chard

1 bunch spring onions (including tops)

½ cup olive oil

2 large onions

2 bunches chives

4 bunches sorrel

2 bunches fennel leaves

salt, cayenne, black pepper

Soak the bulgur wheat for half an hour (see page 3).

Meanwhile, wash the vegetables and herbs, and drain well.

Slice the spinach finely.

Remove the centre rib of each chard leaf and chop the leaves. (Reserve the rib as they can be used in other dishes.)

Coarsely chop chives, sorrel and fennel.

Discard the wilted leaves of spring onions and finely chop both the green tops and the bulbs.

Cut onions into very thin slices.

Heat the olive oil in a large saucepan and fry the onions until they turn golden brown.

Add chopped spinach, chopped chard and spring onions.

Fry on medium heat for 10 more minutes, stirring constantly.

Reduce the heat, add chopped herbs and the bulgur wheat. Fry for a further 10 minutes, stirring.

Add salt, cayenne and black pepper.

Mix well and serve.

CUCUMBER AND TOMATO SALAD

Salatet kyar b-banadura

Preparation time: 20 minutes
SERVES 4

4 tomatoes
4 small cucumbers (or half an ordinary-sized cucumber)
½ bunch parsley
½ bunch fresh mint
1 sprig basil
1 green pimento
salt
1 tsp olive oil

FOR THE GARLIC SAUCE

2 cloves garlic
3 tsp olive oil
1 tsp sherry vinegar (if this is not available, use any good wine vinegar)

Wash the tomatoes, cucumbers and herbs, and leave to drain.

Cut the tomatoes into large cubes, and put into a salad bowl.

Peel and dice the cucumbers and add to the tomatores.

Coarsely chop the mint, parsley and basil.

Thinly slice the pimento.

Prepare a garlic sauce from the garlic, oil and wine vinegar (see page 4).

Pour the garlic sauce over the mixed salad.

Drizzle the teaspoon of olive oil over the top.

Mix and serve immediately.

SAVORY SALAD

Salatet za'atar

Preparation time: 15 minutes
SERVES 2

3 bunches fresh savory*
2 shallots
3 tbsp olive oil
juice of ½ lime
salt
1 tomato

Select the youngest savory leaves, wash and drain.

Finely chop the shallots and place in a salad bowl together with the savory leaves.

Add oil, lime juice and salt.

Using fingertips, gently mix until savory leaves are saturated with oil and lime juice.

Garnish with tomato slices and serve.

* Savory grows wild in the arid Mediterranean countryside, but can equally well be cultivated here as a salad vegetable.

SPINACH WITH RICE

Sbaneg 'a rozz

Preparation time: 30 minutes
Cooking time: 15 minutes
SERVES 4

1 kg (2lb) spinach
50 g (2oz) butter
1 cup long grain rice (basmati or similar)
cinnamon
3/4 cup vermicelli
5 small pots of plain yogurt (preferably goats' milk)
1/2 bunch fresh mint
3 medium cloves of garlic
1/2 cup pine nuts, roasted
salt, pepper

Wash spinach and boil in salted water. When spinach is tender, drain and squeeze out all excess moisture.

Melt 25 g (1oz) butter in a large, heavy-bottomed saucepan and gently sauté the spinach.

Melt the remaining butter in another large, heavy-bottomed saucepan.

Gently sauté the vermicelli in the butter, stirring constantly until it turns golden brown.

Add the rice and continue cooking for another 5–10 minutes while stirring over a moderate heat.

Season with the salt, pepper and cinnamon.

Mix well and add 2 cups of boiling water.

Cover and let boil for 3 to 5 minutes.

Reduce to a moderate heat and allow the rice to swell for a couple of minutes before serving.

Finely grind the garlic and mint.

Mix together yogurt, garlic and mint, then beat the mixture well with a fork.

Place the rice in the middle of a serving dish, surrounded by small mounds of spinach alternating with small heaps of fried pine nuts.

Serve with the yogurt sauce.

POTATOES WITH ONIONS
Batata b-basal

Preparation time: 15 minutes
Cooking time: 15–20 minutes
SERVES 4

---

1 kg (2lb) small potatoes

500 g (1lb) onions

½ cup olive oil

½ tsp paprika

1 bunch spring onions

salt

Wash the potatoes and, without peeling, boil them in water.

Remove skins from the cooked potatoes, then mash them with the back of a fork.

Peel and thinly slice the onions.

Heat oil in a large skillet and lightly brown the sliced onions.

Add the mashed potatoes.

Mix well over heat for 5–7 minutes.

Add salt to taste.

Sprinkle with paprika.

Serve with spring onions.

STUFFED AUBERGINES

Mehsi-batinjan

Preparation time: 1 hour 30 minutes
Cooking time: 1 hour
SERVES 4

1 kg (2lb) small aubergines

FOR THE STUFFING

½ cup rice

3 ripe tomatoes

2 onions

1 bunch parsley

1 cup vegetable oil

salt, pepper, cinnamon

FOR THE STOCK

juice of 2 limes

1 small can of tomato paste

salt, pepper, cinnamon

Wash aubergines and remove a thin slice from the bottom of each one so that they can be firmly stood up in the pan. Soften the aubergines by rolling them between the palms of your hands.

Stand aubergines in a salad bowl, sprinkle salt over their open tops and allow to stand for 10 minutes.

Taking care not to cut through the skin, slowly hollow out the aubergines until no flesh remains. Set the flesh aside on a plate.

THE STUFFING

Wash and finely chop the parsley.

Wash and dice tomatoes.

Mince onions.

Wash rice thoroughly, drain and place in a large mixing bowl.

Add parsley, tomatoes, onions, oil, salt, pepper, cinnamon and mix together.

Stuff the aubergines until half-full only, so that they don't split open when the rice swells.

THE STOCK

Fill a large heavy-bottomed saucepan with 1 litre (1¾ pints) of water. Add salt, pepper, cinnamon, lime juice, tomato paste and bring to the boil.

Plug the open top of the aubergine with a piece of tomato or a firm piece of the aubergine flesh, then carefully place them in the saucepan with the stock.

Cook over a moderate heat for 40–50 minutes. Using a skimmer, push aubergines back down in the stock from time to time.

When the aubergines are cooked, quickly remove them from the saucepan and arrange on a serving dish.

SAUTÉED POTATOES
Batata mhar'sa

Preparation time: 10 minutes
Cooking time: 15 minutes
SERVES 4

---

1 kg (2lb) very small new potatoes

FOR THE GARLIC SAUCE

5 cloves garlic

½ cup olive oil

juice of 3 limes

salt

Scrub the potatoes and wash thoroughly until the skins are smooth and almost translucent.

Leave to drain in a colander, then wipe dry with a cloth.

Prepare a garlic sauce with oil, garlic and lime juice (see page 4).

Heat the oil in a large skillet and add the unpeeled potatoes.

Fry potatoes, shaking the pan every 2–3 minutes. The skins of the potatoes will wrinkle while they are frying.

When they turn golden, pour in the garlic sauce.

Mix well, season to taste, serve hot.

PURSLANE SALAD

Salatet ba'leh

Preparation time: 20 minutes
SERVES 4

3 bunches purslane
½ bunch fresh mint
½ bunch parsley
2 cloves garlic
1 tbsp sherry vinegar (if not available, any good wine vinegar may be used)
2 tbsp olive oil
salt
1 tomato

Select the best purslane leaves, discarding the wilted leaves and stems.

Wash and drain the purslane leaves.

Wash and drain the mint leaves.

Wash the parsley. Discard stalks and tough leaves, and coarsely chop the remainder.

Grind the garlic as described on page 4.

Mix together the ground garlic with the vinegar and pour the sauce over the purslane, mint and parsley leaves.

Add olive oil and mix well, using fingers, until leaves are saturated with the sauce.

Serve garnished with slices of tomato.

POTATOES WITH CORIANDER

Batata b-kozbra

Preparation time: 15 minutes
Cooking time: 20 minutes
SERVES 4

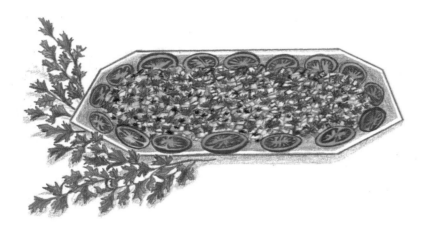

500 g (1lb) new potatoes
6 tbsp olive oil
2 bunches coriander
2 medium cloves garlic
1 lemon
salt
1 tomato

Peel, wash and dice the potatoes into 2 cm (³/₄ inch) cubes.

Heat oil in a large skillet and add the potatoes when oil is sizzling hot.

Cover the pan for a second and shake. Uncover pan immediately.

Shake the pan every 2 minutes until the potatoes are golden brown all over.

Meanwhile, wash the coriander, pat dry and chop coarsely.

Grind the garlic until very smooth

When the potatoes are golden brown, mix in the ground garlic, the lemon juice and the chopped coriander.

Stir over heat for 2 or 3 minutes.

Serve garnished with slices of tomato.

POTATO STEW

Batata b-dammu

Preparation time: 20 minutes
Cooking time: 45 minutes
SERVES 4

1 kg (2lb) new potatoes
1 kg (2lb) ripe tomatoes
2 large onions
½ cup olive oil
½ head garlic
salt
1 sprig parsley
black pepper

Peel and dice the potatoes.

Peel tomatoes, remove seeds, and dice.

Peel and very thinly slice the onions.

Peel garlic, leaving cloves whole.

Heat the oil in a large, heavy-bottomed saucepan and stir-fry the onions until golden brown.

Mix in the tomatoes and the peeled cloves of garlic.

Add salt to taste and cook covered over a moderate heat for 15 minutes.

Add the potatoes, cover the pan and simmer over a low heat for 30–40 minutes. If the tomatoes do not make sufficient juice, ½ cup water may be added.

Once the potatoes are cooked, add black pepper, mix well, sprinkle with chopped parsley, and serve.

(The garlic cloves can be removed before serving, according to taste.)

POTATOES WITH PAPRIKA
Batata mlafha

Preparation time: 20 minutes
Cooking time: 15 minutes
SERVES 4

500 g (1lb) new potatoes
500 g (1lb) onions
1 cup ground nut oil
salt, pepper
1 tsp paprika

Peel, wash and thinly slice the potatoes.

Cut onions into very thin slices.

Heat the oil in a large skillet and gently sauté the onions over a moderate heat until golden brown.

Add the potatoes to the pan and mix carefully, so that the potato skins do not break.

Simmer for 20 minutes, shaking the pan frequently.

When cooked the potatoes should still be firm.

Season with salt and pepper.

Sprinkle with paprika and serve.

TOMATO AND ONION SALAD

Salatet banadura b-basal

> *Preparation time:* 15 minutes
> SERVES 4

3 medium tomatoes
2 Spanish onions
2 sprigs basil
juice of ½ lime
3 tbsp olive oil
salt

Wash the tomatoes and cut into small cubes.

Mince the onions and chop the basil.

Season with the lime juice and olive oil.

Add salt to taste, mix well and serve.

This salad is often served together with dishes such as mjadra with lentils and mjadra with red beans.

POTATO KEBBEH

Kebbet batata

Preparation time: 30 minutes
Cooking time: (potatoes) 20 minutes
SERVES 4

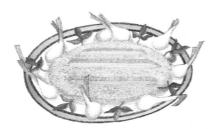

½ cup of fine bulgur wheat
500 g (1lb) new potatoes
1 bunch fresh mint, washed and dried
1 large onion
1 green pimento
½ tsp each: cinnamon, black pepper
a pinch cayenne
salt
2 tbsp olive oil
1 bunch spring onions

Soak the bulgur wheat for 15–20 minutes (see page 3).

Wash the potatoes and, without peeling, boil under tender.

Remove potato skins and purée the potatoes in a blender.

In a mortar, separately grind the mint (keeping back a few leaves for garnish), then the onions, then the green pimento.

Mix together mint, onions, green pimento and spices.

Add salt and mix in the puréed potatoes.

Add the soaked bulgur wheat and knead the mixture with your hands, moistening it with a few drops of cold water.

Using fingers, make a few small hollows in the mixture, and fill them with olive oil.

Serve decorated with mint leaves and accompanied by spring onions.

BAKED POTATO KEBBEH

Kebbet batata bes-sayniyyeh

> *Preparation time:* 45 minutes
> *Cooking time:* 45 minutes
> + 2 hours soaking for bulgur wheat
> + overnight soaking for chickpeas
> SERVES 4

FOR THE DOUGH

1½ cups fine bulgur wheat
4 medium potatoes
½ bunch mint
1 large onion
2 tbsp flour
½ tsp each: cinnamon, paprika salt, pepper

FOR THE FILLING

4 medium onions ground nut oil
½ cup dried chickpeas
pinch cinnamon
1 tbsp sugar
salt, pepper

IN ADVANCE

Soak and prepare the chickpeas overnight (see page 5).

Soak the bulgur wheat for 2 hours in advance.

DOUGH

Without peeling, wash the potatoes and boil in salted water until tender.

Remove potato skins and purée the flesh in a blender.

Wash and pat dry the mint leaves. Discard stalks.

Grind the mint leaves and onions.

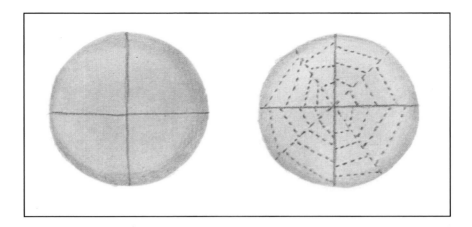

Mix together the ground onion, mint, spices, salt and bulgur wheat. Mix well.

Add the puréed potatoes and knead the dough until soft and smooth.

FILLING

Prepare a basal mhammar with the onions and oil (see page 9).

Remove onions from oil and add to prepared chickpeas.

Season with pepper and cinnamon. Mix well.

Preheat a moderate oven.

Spread a layer of the dough, a few millimetres thick, on the bottom of a greased baking dish (the dough can be moistened and briefly rekneaded if it has become too dry.

Cover with a layer of filling.

Top with another thin layer of dough.

Using a knife, trace two lines to form a cross on the surface of the dough, then cut along these lines right through the layers (letting the knife reach the bottom of the baking dish).

Then trace other lines, on the surface only, to form a lattice patterns (see illustration); this time, take care not to let the knife go through to the bottom.

Brush the surface with the ground nut oil, place in the preheated oven and bake at a moderate heat until golden (25-30 minutes).

Serve warm or cold.

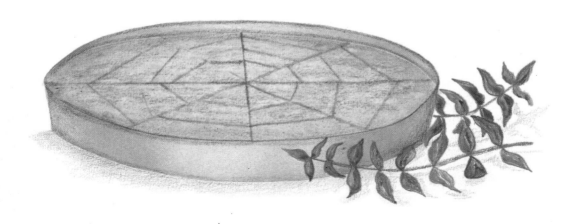

STUFFED COURGETTES
Mehsi kusa

Preparation time: 1 hour 30 minutes
Cooking time: 1 hour +
overnight soaking for the chickpeas
SERVES 4

FOR THE STUFFING

½ cup dried chickpeas

1 cup rice

2 tomatoes bunch parsley

½ bunch fresh mint

bunch chives

2 shallots

4 tbsp olive oil

salt, pepper

1 kg (2lb) small courgettes

salt

1 head garlic

½ tsp each: paprika, cinnamon, pepper

juice of 4 lemons

1 lemon, sliced

IN ADVANCE

Soak chickpeas overnight (see page 5).

THE STUFFING

The next day, prepare chickpeas.

Wash rice well and drain off in a strainer.

Wash parsley, chives and tomatoes, and pat dry with a cloth.

Finely chop the herbs (set aside 1 tbsp chopped parsley), dice the tomatoes and mince the shallots.

Put the rice, herbs, chickpeas, tomatoes and shallots together in a salad bowl and mix together.

Add salt, pepper, spices and oil, and mix well.

Wash the courgettes well and cut off the stalks.

Dip the open end of courgettes into the salt and stand them, open ends up, in a salad bowl.

Scoop out the flesh of the courgettes, scraping the insides with slow, regular strokes until no flesh remains. Take care not to cut through the skin.

Set the flesh aside on a plate.

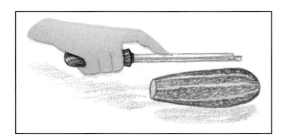

Wash the hollowed-out courgettes in salted water and shake well to remove any remaining pulp.

Half-fill each courgette with the prepared stuffing. It is important only to half-fill courgettes so that they do not burst open when the rice swells with cooking.

Plug the openings of the courgettes with a slice of tomato, or a slice of courgette.

Put 2 litres (3½ pints) of water in a large heavy-bottomed saucepan.

Add salt, the juice of 4 lemons, 1 tbsp chopped parsley and ½ cup of the courgette flesh and bring to the boil.

When the water is boiling, add the courgettes one by one.

Half cover the saucepan and cook over a moderate heat for 20 minutes. Then reduce heat and cook for a further 40 minutes.

Grind the garlic, as described on page 4, and add to the stock with the courgettes.

Cook for 2–3 minutes, then quickly remove the courgettes from the stock.

Place courgettes onto a serving dish and garnish with slices of lemon.

Serve warm or cold.

BEETROOT AND WHITE CABBAGE SALAD

Salatet smandar w-malfuf

Preparation time: 20 minutes
SERVES 4

1 small head white cabbage

2 medium beetroots

25 g (1oz) crushed walnuts

salt

FOR GARLIC SAUCE

2 limes

2 cloves garlic

3 tbsp ground nut oil

Discard the wilted outer cabbage leaves.

Trim off the centre rib of each leaf and cut both cabbage and beetroot into very thin slices.

Prepare a garlic sauce with the lemon juice, oil and garlic (see page 4) and pour over the sliced cabbage and beetroot.

Add salt and mix.

Garnish with crushed walnuts and serve.

FRIED FAVA BEANS

Ful m'alla

Preparation time: 20 minutes
Cooking time: 40 minutes
SERVES 4

1 kg (2lb) green fava beans (young broad beans)
3 large onions
½ cup olive oil
2 ripe tomatoes
2 cloves garlic
salt
½ tsp cumin
½ tsp cinnamon
a pinch cayenne
1 bunch spring onions

String green fava beans, remove the stalks, and cut into 1 cm (½ inch) pieces. Wash and drain.

Peel the onions and cut into very thin slices.

Peel and coarsely chop the tomatoes.

Heat the oil in a large heavy-bottomed saucepan and sauté the onions until golden brown.

Add the beans and tomatoes, and stir-fry for 20 minutes.

Add coarsely chopped garlic, salt and enough water to cover the vegetables.

Cover the pan and cook over a moderate heat until all the water has evaporated.

Taste to check. If not cooked add some boiling water and cook for a few more minutes.

When beans are cooked, turn off the heat, season with the spices and mix.

Serve warm or cold with spring onions.

POTATO SALAD

Salatet batata

Preparation time: 20 minutes
Cooking time: (potatoes) 20 minutes
SERVES 1–2

4 large new potatoes
2 large tomatoes
½ bunch fresh mint
½ bunch parsley
1 bunch chives
juice of 1 lemon
½ cup olive oil
salt, cayenne, black pepper
1 lettuce

Wash the unpeeled potatoes and boil in salted water.

Meanwhile, wash and drain mint, tomatoes, parsley and chives.

When the potatoes are done, peel and dice them.

Chop the chives and mint and dice the tomatoes into 2 cm (1 inch) thick cubes.

In a salad bowl, mix together the olive oil, lemon juice, salt, cayenne and black pepper.

Add the potato cubes, tomatoes and herbs.

Gently mix all the ingredients together, season to taste and serve on a bed of crispy lettuce leaves.

CABBAGE AND TOMATO SALAD

Salatet malfuf b-banadura

Preparation time: 20 minutes
SERVES 4

1 head white cabbage
3 tomatoes
3 tbsp olive oil
2 small limes
3 cloves garlic
salt

Detach all cabbage leaves.

Gather the leaves into a bunch and cut into very thin slices.

Wash and dice the tomatoes.

Using the oil, juice of 1 lime, and the garlic cloves, prepare a garlic sauce (see page 4).

Mix all ingredients together in a salad bowl.

Add salt and 3 tbsp oil.

Mix well and serve garnished with thin slices of lime.

POTATO AND BULGUR WHEAT PATTIES
Sraysira

Preparation time: 1 hour
Cooking time: 30 minutes
SERVES 6

3 cups fine bulgur wheat

1 kg (2lb) potatoes

2 large onions

1 bunch fresh mint

1 tsp each: paprika, cayenne, cinnamon,
black pepper

salt

1 cup olive oil

1 cos lettuce

Soak the bulgur wheat for a good 2 hours.

Boil the unpeeled potatoes in salted water.
Potatoes must remain firm.

Meanwhile, wash the mint, chop the onions
and grind them together in a mortar.

Mash the potatoes and season with spices
and salt.

Mix the potatoes with the bulgur wheat.

Knead the mixture for 10 minutes.

Shape the mixture into patties 1 cm ($\frac{1}{2}$
inch) thick and 10 cm (5 inches) long.

Place on a lightly floured baking dish and
bake in the preheated oven until they turn
golden brown on both sides.

One by one, dip the baked patties into a
bowl of olive oil.

Serve cold with salad of cos lettuce.

IN ADVANCE (IF PRESERVED VINE
LEAVES ARE USED)*

Remove the stalks from the vine leaves and soak them in water to remove salt.

Change water twice and then once or twice again the following day before preparing the stuffing.

THE STUFFING

Add half a cup of water to the bulgur wheat.

Mix until grains are all well moistened.

Wash, dry and finely chop the herbs. Add them to the bulgur wheat.

Peel and mince the onion and add to the other ingredients.

Peel the tomato, remove seed, dice and add to the bulgur wheat.

Add salt, pepper, spices, oil and lemon juice. Mix well.

Lay out the leaves on a wooden board (shiny side down) and spread a teaspoon of filling on each leaf.

Fold the left and right sides of the vine leaf and then the base (stem-end) over the filling.

Then carefully roll the leaf away from you to form a cigar-shaped package.

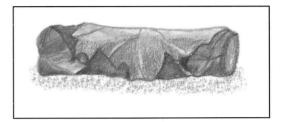

Arrange the vine rolls side by side at the bottom of a pot then add another layer of rolls on top of them. Continue adding in layers until all rolls are used up.

Lay a plate upside-down, over the top layer.** Press down with a spoon and add enough boiling water to cover the plate.

Lift the plate slightly and add olive oil. Cover and bring to the boil.

Reduce to a moderate heat for ¼ hour.

Finally, reduce to a low heat and cook until done (20–30 minutes).

Serve warm or cold.

* This dish will taste even better if fresh vine leaves are used. Choose fresh, small and tender ones, wash them thoroughly, and blanch them for one or two minutes in boiling water.

** Choose a plate that is big enough to cover all the vine leaves, but that is also small enough to be removed easily. The plate is left on top of the vine leaves until they're done to prevent the rolls from bursting open.

STUFFED CHARD

Mehsi sale

Preparation time: 1 hour 40 minutes
Cooking time: 40 minutes
+ overnight soaking for chickpeas
SERVES 4

1 kg (2lb) chard
juice of 2 lemons
4 tbsp olive oil
salt

FOR THE STUFFING
½ cup dried chickpeas
1 cup short grain rice
juice of 1 lemon
2 bunches parsley
1 bunch fresh mint
1 bunch chives
1 onion
5 tbsp olive oil
½ tsp each: salt, pepper, paprika, cinnamon
a pinch cayenne

IN ADVANCE

Pick over the chickpeas and soak in water overnight (see page 5).

THE STUFFING

Wash the rice, drain and put in a bowl.

Wash the herbs, wipe dry with a cloth, chop finely and add to the rice.

Mince the onion and add to the rice and herbs.

Pour the oil and lemon juice over the rice mixture.

Add chickpeas.

Add salt and spices. Mix all the ingredients together well.

ASSEMBLY

Choosing the small, tender and untorn chard leaves, wash and separate ribs from the leaves (see illustrations on pages 52–53).

Blanch leaves in boiling water for 2 minutes, then rinse under cold water and drain.

Spread leaves out on a wooden board, shiny sides down.

Place a teaspoon of filling on each leaf and spread it to within 1 cm (¹/₂ inch) of the edges of the leaf.

Fold the base of the leaf over the filling and roll (see illustrations on pages 52–53). Reserve the stalks of the chards as they can be used in other dishes.

Line the bottom of a large heavy-bottomed saucepan with 2 or 3 leaves.

Tightly pack the stuffed leaves side by side and build in layers.

Lay a plate upside-down over the top layer.*

Press down with a wooden spoon or spatula and add enough boiling water to cover the plate by 1 cm (¹/₂ inch).

Lift the plate slightly and add the juice of 2 lemons and 4 tablespoons of olive oil.

Sprinkle with a pinch of salt and cover.

Bring to the boil, then reduce to a moderate heat and cook for 15 minutes.

Finally, simmer gently for a further 10 minutes or until done.

Serve warm or cold.

* Choose a plate that is big enough to cover all the chard leaves, but that is also small enough to be removed easily. The plate should be left in position throughout the cooking time to prevent the rolls from bursting.

VINE LEAVES STUFFED WITH RICE
Mehsi wara'inab b-rozz

Preparation time: 1 hour 40 minutes
Cooking time: 45 minutes
+ overnight soaking if using preserved
vine leaves
SERVES 4

---

500 g (1lb) vine leaves

4 tbsp olive oil

FOR THE STUFFING

1 cup short grain rice

1 lemon

1 tomato

1 bunch parsley

1/2 bunch fresh mint

1 bunch chives

1/4 cup olive oil

1/2 tsp each: salt, pepper, paprika, cinnamon

a pinch cayenne

FOR THE TOMATO AND ONION MIXTURE

500 g (1lb) ripe tomatoes

3 onions

1 lemon

4 tbsp olive oil

salt

IN ADVANCE (IF USING PRESERVED VINE LEAVES)*

Remove stalks from the vine leaves.

Soak them in water to remove salt.

Change water twice then again once or twice the following day before preparing the stuffing.

THE STUFFING

Wash and drain rice and place in a large heavy-bottomed saucepan.

Wash and finely chop the herbs.

Wash the tomato, wipe dry with a cloth and dice into small cubes.

Add the herbs and diced tomatoes to the rice.

Season with salt and spices.

Add oil and lemon juice, and mix well together.

THE TOMATO AND ONION MIXTURE

Peel onions, chop coarsely and fry in oil until they turn golden brown.

Peel and dice the tomatoes, remove seeds and stir into pan with the onions.

50

Add salt and fry tomatoes and onions for 12 minutes over a low heat.

Set the mixture aside on a plate.

ASSEMBLY

Spread the vine leaves out on a wooden board (shiny side down).

Place a teaspoon of filling in the centre of each leaf.

Fold the base (stem-end) over the filling, then fold the right and left sides over and roll away from you to make a cigar-shaped package. Stuff all the vine leaves in this way.

Arrange a layer of stuffed vine leaves at the bottom of a large heavy-bottomed sauce-pan and spread the tomato and onion mixture over them.

Cover the mixture with another tightly-packed layer of vine leaves and continue to add layers until all the vine leaves have been used up.

Place a plate upside-down over the top layer. The plate should remain in place throughout the cooking time.**

Press down with a wooden spoon or spatula and add enough boiling water to cover by 2 cm (1 inch).

Slightly lift the plate and add olive oil, cover and bring to the boil.

Reduce to a moderate heat and cook for ¼ hour.

Reduce to a low heat and cook until done (30-40 minutes). If necessary, add ½ cup of boiling water and cook for a few more minutes.

Serve hot, warm or cold.

* This delicious dish will taste even better if fresh vine leaves are used. Choose fresh, small and tender ones, wash them thoroughly and blanch them for one or two minutes in boiling water.

** Choose a plate that is big enough to cover all the vine leaves, but that is also small enough to be removed easily. The plate is left over the vine leaves throughout the cooking time to prevent rolls from bursting open.

CABBAGE STUFFED WITH BULGUR WHEAT
Mehsi malfuf b-burgul

Preparation time: 1 hour 30 minutes
Cooking time: 40 minutes
SERVES 4

1 medium cabbage (white or green)

4 tbsp olive oil

salt

½ head garlic

3–4 lemons

FOR THE STUFFING

1 cup coarse bulgur wheat

1 onion

2 bunches parsley

½ bunch fresh mint

1 bunch chives

½ tsp each: salt, cinnamon, paprika.

4 tbsp olive oil

THE STUFFING

Pour ½ cup of water over bulgur wheat.

Using fingers, mix until all grains are moistened.

Add the finely chopped onion, parsley, mint and chives.

Finely chop the onions and add to the bulgur wheat.

Add salt and spices.

Add the oil and mix together.

Boil 2–3 litres (3½–5 pints) of water in a large, heavy-bottomed saucepan.

Blanch cabbage in boiling water for 2–3 minutes.

Remove cabbage from water and cut off the leaves that have softened.

Return the remainder of the cabbage with the leaves that are still hard to the water for a further 2–3 minutes. Repeat this process until all the leaves have softened.

Separate the centre ribs from each leaf. The ribs will be used later on in this recipe.

Spread out the cabbage leaves on a wooden board.

Place a teaspoon of filling in the centre of each leaf and spread it to within 1 cm ($\frac{1}{2}$ inch) from the edges of the leaf.

Fold the base of the leaf over the filling and roll away from you.

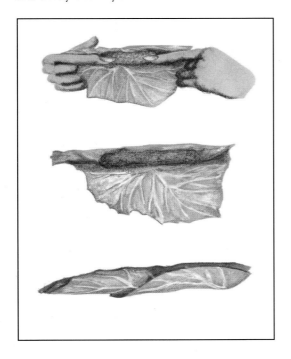

Stuff and roll all the leaves in this way.

Place a layer of cabbage ribs on the bottom of a large heavy-bottomed saucepan.

Arrange the stuffed leaves side by side and in layers.

Plate a plate, upside-down, over the top layer.*

Press the plate down with a wooden spoon or spatula, and add enough boiling water to cover the plate by 2 cm (1 inch).

Lift the plate slightly and add 4 tablespoons of oil.

Sprinkle with a pinch of salt.

Cover and bring to the boil.

Reduce to a moderate heat for $\frac{1}{4}$ hour.

Finally simmer over low heat until cooked (20–25 minutes).

Prick a stuffed leaf with a fork to check if cooked. If necessary add $\frac{1}{2}$ cup of boiling water and simmer for a few minutes more.

Grind the garlic and prepare a garlic sauce (see page 4). Thin down with the juice of two of the lemons and pour over the cabbage leaves.

Shake the saucepan.

Simmer for about 2-3 minutes and then remove from heat.

Serve on a dish, garnished with slices of the remaining lemon.

* Choose a plate that is big enough to cover all the stuffed leaves, but that is also small enough to be removed easily. The plate is left over the cabbage leaves throughout the cooking time to prevent rolls from bursting open.

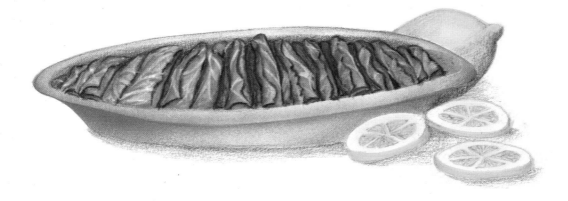

OKRA WITH OIL

Bamyeh b-zeit

Preparation time: 40 minutes
Cooking time: 45 minutes
SERVES 6

1 kg (2lb) okra
500 g (1lb) ripe tomatoes
500 g (1lb) small onions
½ cup ground nut oil
salt, pepper

Cut off the stalk at the base of the okra pods.

Wash and drain.

Wash tomatoes, peel and remove seeds.

Peel onions, and put them whole into a heavy-bottomed saucepan.

Gently sauté the onions in oil.

Stir in the tomatoes.

Heat oil in a skillet and fry the okra (okra should be fried in small quantities so that they turn golden brown on all sides).

Once okra is fried, add the onions and tomatoes.

Mix well together and season with salt and pepper.

Cover with water and simmer covered for 10 minutes over a moderate heat.

Reduce heat and simmer until all of the water evaporates (20–30 minutes).

PUMPKIN KEBBEH

Kebbet jlannt

Preparation time: 30 minutes
Cooking time: 45 minutes
+ overnight soaking for chickpeas
SERVES 6

½ cup dried chickpeas
1 kg (2lb) pumpkin
1½ cups fine bulgur wheat
2 large onions
½ bunch fresh mint
3 tbsp flour
½ tbsp sweet pimento
a pinch cayenne
½ tsp cinnamon
salt
2 tbsp caster sugar
1 cos lettuce
oil

Finely chop the onions.

Wash the mint and pat dry.

Add the mint, chopped onions and flour to the pumpkin and bulgur wheat mixture.

Season with salt and spices.

Knead the mixture and add the chickpeas.

In a lightly-greased baking dish spread the mixture to form a layer no thicker than 1 cm (½ inch).

Trace the lines across the surface of the kebbeh as indicated in the kebbeh batata recipe (pages 36–37).

Sprinkle with two tablespoons of sugar.

Pour on enough oil to cover the mixture.

Bake in a moderate oven for 30-40 minutes.

Serve warm or cold with cos lettuce.

Soak the chickpeas overnight (see page 5).

Preheat a moderate oven.

Cut the pumpkin into large cubes and boil in water for 15-20 minutes.

Drain cubes off in a colander.

Mash the cut pumpkin and add to the bulgur wheat (bulgur wheat should not be soaked).

Mix and leave to stand.

SPINACH KEBBEH

Kebbeh bes-sbaneg

Preparation time: 1 hour 30 minutes
Cooking time: 40 minutes
SERVES 4

FOR THE DOUGH

1 cup flour
1 cup fine bulgur wheat
1 small onion
½ tsp paprika
a pinch pepper
½ tsp each: cinnamon, cumin
salt

1 kg (2lb) fresh spinach
4 onions
½ cup oil
salt, pepper
½ tsp cayenne

THE DOUGH

Mix the flour, bulgur wheat, spices, salt and finely chopped onions.

Add ½ cup of water to this mixture.

Knead the dough, adding a few drops of water if needed.

Keep kneading until the dough is soft and smooth.

Take small pieces of dough and roll between your palms, then flatten out by squashing them with your fingers against your palm. Shape into small flat cakes. If the dough hardens, add a few drops of water and knead again.

Sprinkle a large baking dish with flour and place the flat cakes in the dish.

Boil 2 litres (3½ pints) water in a heavy-bottomed saucepan. Add salt.

Carefully put the flat cakes into the boiling water and cook over moderate heat for 20 minutes. Drain off in a colander.

Remove stalks from spinach, wash and boil in water.

Pour the cooked spinach in a colander, rinse out in cold water and drain.

Prepare a basal mhammar with the oil and onions (see page 9).

Squeeze out all excess moisture from spinach and add, stirring, to the fried onions.

Stir-fry constantly for 5 minutes, then add the well-drained kebbeh. Stir-fry on high for a few more minutes.

Add salt and pepper.

Serve, sprinkled with cayenne.

GRILLED AUBERGINES WITH GARLIC

Baba gannuj

Preparation time: 15 minutes
Cooking time: 20 minutes
SERVES 4

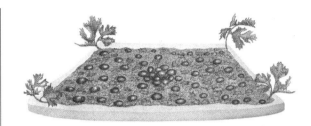

2 large aubergines

1 large clove garlic

olive oil

1 green pimento

2 sprigs parsley

1 pomegranate

salt

Grill the aubergines over wood or charcoal. If possible, prepare the fire with pine cones If no barbecue is available, grill the aubergines conventionally - you can char the skins directly over the gas flame. Turn so they cook evenly.

Peel the burnt skin from the aubergine.

Leave the drain off for a few minutes.

Mash the flesh of the aubergines.

Prepare a garlic sauce with the oil and garlic (see page 4).

Mix together the garlic sauce and the mashed aubergines.

Mash the mixture again and mix in the finely chopped green pimento. Salt to taste.

Spread the mixture out onto a serving dish, sprinkle with pomegranate seeds, and garnish with the chopped parsley. Dot with a few drops of oil before serving.

MIXED SALAD

Salata msakleh

Preparation time: 20 minutes
SERVES 6

1 bunch purslane
½ bunch parsley
½ bunch fresh mint
1 green pimento
½ cucumber
3 large tomatoes
3 cloves garlic
2 tbsp wine vinegar
4 tbsp olive oil
salt

Pluck off the purslane leaves.

Wash and drain them.

Wash the parsley, mint, pimento and cucumber, and pat dry.

Coarsely chop the parsley and mint.

Finely chop the pimento.

Peel the cucumber.

Dice the tomatoes and cucumber.

Mix all these ingredients together in a salad bowl.

Prepare a garlic sauce with the garlic, oil and vinegar (see page 4).

Pour the sauce over the salad.

Add salt.

Mix well and serve.

CAULIFLOWER WITH SESAME CREAM
Arnabit me'li

Preparation time: 30 minutes
Cooking time: 30 minutes
SERVES 6

1 cauliflower
1 cup ground-nut oil
GARLIC SAUCE PREPARED WITH:
1 lime
3 cloves garlic
oil
2 tbsp sesame cream
2 sprig parsley
50 g (2oz) pine nuts

Divide the cauliflower into small florets and wash.

Boil in salted water for 10 minutes.

Rinse in cold water and drain.

Heat one cup of ground nut oil in a large skillet and stir-fry the cauliflower.

Remove and drain on a paper towel.

Put the fried cauliflower onto a plate.

Prepare a garlic sauce with the oil, garlic and lime juice (see page 4).

Mix this sauce with the sesame cream (see instructions page 6).

Pour the mixture over the cauliflower.

Serve sprinkled with finely chopped parsley and grilled pine nuts.

MIXED VEGETABLES
Alib kodra

Preparation time: 20 minutes
Cooking time: 1 hour
SERVES 6

2 onions
250 g (½lb) green beans
1 carrot
1 pimento
2 ripe medium tomatoes
1 medium potatoes
1 aubergine
1 courgette
½ cup oil
½ cup water
1 tsp each salt, cayenne, black pepper

String the beans and cut into halves.

Peel the other vegetables and cut into thin slices.

Heat the oil in a large heavy-bottomed saucepan and sauté the onion slices.

Remove from heat when golden brown on all sides.

Place a layer of green beans over the onions, then cover with successive layers of sliced tomatoes.

Mix together in a bowl the water, salt, pepper and cayenne.

Pour the liquid over the vegetables.

Cover and bring to the boil.

Reduce to a moderate heat and simmer for about an hour.

Serve hot.

GRILLED AUBERGINES WITH SESAME CREAM
Matabbal

Preparation time: 20 minutes
Cooking time: 20 minutes
SERVES 4

2 large aubergines
1 tbsp tahini
2 medium cloves garlic
½ lemon
salt
½ pomegranate
2 sprigs parsley
2 tbsp olive oil

Grill the aubergines (see page 56).

Add a few drops of water to the tahini and beat until very smooth (see page 6).

Grind the garlic.

Mix together the crushed garlic, sesame cream and the grilled and mashed aubergines.

Add the juice of half a lemon.

Add salt to taste and mix well.

Spread mixture onto a serving dish.

Sprinkle with pomegranate seeds and garnish with chopped parsley.

Drizzle the olive oil on top and serve.

FRIED AUBERGINES

Batinjan me'li

Preparation time: 15 minutes
Cooking time: 15 minutes
SERVES 2

| 2 large aubergines |
| salt |
| oil for frying |
| 1 large tomato |

FOR GARLIC SAUCE

| 1 lemon |
| 3 cloves garlic |
| 3 tbsp olive oil |

Wash the aubergines and peel removing only part of the skin in strips.

Cut lengthwise into slices 1 cm ($\frac{1}{2}$ inch) thick.

Sprinkle with salt and leave to stand for at least half an hour.

Pat dry on a paper towel.

Heat oil in a large skillet and lightly brown the sliced aubergines on both sides.

Put onto a serving dish.

Garnish with slices of tomatoes.

Serve with a garlic sauce (see page 4).

CHARD RIBS WITH SESAME CREAM
Dla'sale'b-thineh

Preparation time: 20 minutes
Cooking time: 30 minutes
SERVES 4

1 kg (2lb) of central ribs from chard leaves
juice of 2 lemons
1½ tbsp tahini
4 cloves garlic
salt
½ cup crushed walnuts
50 g (2oz) pine nuts
olive oil

String and wash the leaf ribs. (The leaves can be used in preparing another dish.)

Chop the ribs.

Meanwhile bring 2 litres (3½ pints) water to the boil and add the chopped ribs.

Boil the leaf ribs for 30 minutes.

Check that the ribs are tender with the back of a fork. They should be soft and should break easily.

Drain and squeeze out all the excess moisture.

Prepare a sesame cream with the lemon juice and tahini (see page 6).

Grind the garlic and mix with the sesame cream.

Pour the sauce over the ribs and mix well.

Add salt.

Sprinkle with the crushed walnuts and fried pine nuts.

Sprinkle with olive oil and serve.

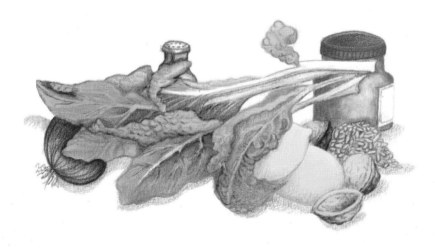

CHARD RIBS WITH CHICKPEAS

Dla'sale m'elleyeh

Preparation time: 20 minutes
Cooking time: 35 minutes
+ overnight soaking for the chickpeas
SERVES 4

½ cup dried chickpeas
1 kg (2lb) central ribs from chard leaves
2 large onions
4 tbsp oil
salt, pepper
½ cup water
½ tsp cinnamon

Soak chickpeas overnight (see page 5).

String the leaf ribs, wash and cut them into pieces 2–3 cm (1 inch) long.

Peel and slice the onions.

Heat oil in a pressure-cooker and fry the slices of onions until golden brown.

Add the pieces of chard ribs.

Stir-fry for 5–10 minutes.

Add the chickpeas.

Add salt, pepper, and ½ cup of water.

Bring the pan up to pressure and cook over a low heat for 20 minutes.

Remove from heat, reduce pressure and allow to cool for 5 minutes before opening the pressure-cooker.

Sprinkle with cinnamon and serve.

CHARD LEAVES WITH BLACK-EYED BEANS

Sale'a lubyeh

> *Preparation time:* 30 minutes
> *Cooking time:* 1 hour 15 minutes
> SERVES 4

---

1 kg (2lb) chards

1 cup black-eyed beans

3 large onions

$^{1}/_{2}$ cup oil

$^{1}/_{2}$ tsp paprika

salt, pepper

Wash the chards and separate the ribs from the leaves.

String the chard ribs and chop into 1 cm ($^{1}/_{2}$ inch) pieces.

Wash the black-eyed beans.

Cook separately in salted water, the beans, ribs and leaves, for 40 minutes, 20 minutes and 10 minutes respectively.

Drain well.

Squeeze out all the excess moisture from the chard leaves.

Using the onions and oil, prepare the basal mhammar in a large skillet (see page 9).

Add the beans and chard, season with salt and pepper, and cook on high for a few minutes, stirring constantly.

Sprinkle with paprika and serve.

SPINACH TURNOVERS

Ftayer bes-sbaneg

Preparation time: 1 hour 30 minutes
Cooking time: 20 minutes
Serves 4

2 ripe tomatoes	
1 small onion	
salt, cayenne, cinnamon, black pepper	
½ cup olive oil	
2 lemons	
1 small bunch chards	
1 kg (2lb) spinach	
1 bunch parsley	
1 bunch fresh mint	
1 bunch chives	

FOR THE DOUGH

250 g (9oz) plain flour
2 tbsp oil
salt
½ tsp dried yeast
½ cup water

THE DOUGH

Put the flour in a large bowl and make a well in the centre.

Pour in the oil, add a pinch of salt.

Work together with your fingers.

Dissolve the yeast in a little of the water, and sprinkle over the mixture.

Add remaining flour and knead thoroughly until a smooth dough is formed.

Cover the dough and leave in a warm place for an hour or until it has doubled in volume.

THE STUFFING

Wash all the vegetables and herbs and drain well.

Wipe dry with cloth.

Finely chop the vegetables, herbs, tomatoes and onions.

Add salt, oil, spices and the juice of ½ lemon.

Mix the ingredients together well.

ASSEMBLING

Roll out the dough and cut out very thin flat cakes about 20 cm (10 inches) in diameter.

Place 2 heaped teaspoons of the spinach mixture in the centre of each flat cake.

Fold the edges over the filling to make a triangle.

Press edges over the filling to make a triangle.

Press edges tightly together to stop them from opening while baking.

Heat the oil in a skillet and fry the ftayer until they turn golden brown on both sides.

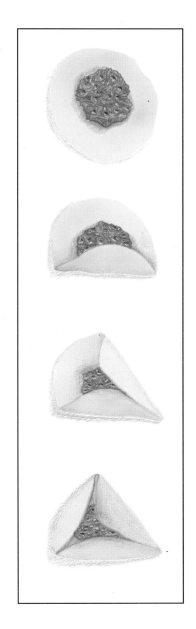

Drain the fried ftayer on a paper towel.

Serve hot with a slice of lemon.

BREAD SALAD

Fattus

Preparation time: 25 minutes
SERVES 4

1 loaf of Lebanese bread (pitta bread)
3 cloves garlic
2 large tomatoes
½ cucumber
1 bunch parsley
½ bunch fresh mint
1 sprig basil
1 onion
1 tsp (Jerez) wine vinegar
1 tbsp olive oil
1 tsp sumac (available from oriental foodstores)
salt

Pre-heat the oven for toasting the bread.

Wash and drain all the vegetables and herbs.

Grind the garlic as indicated on page 4.

Toast the bread, whole, in the oven.

Allow bread to cool and break into 2 cm (1 inch) pieces.

Cut the tomatoes and cucumber into small cubes.

Coarsely chop the parsley, mint, basil and onions.

Mix the pieces of bread with the vegetables.

Pour the garlic, vinegar and oil over the bread and vegetable mixture.

Add salt and mix carefully.

Sprinkle with sumac and serve.

DANDELIONS WITH GARLIC

Hendbeh b-zeit w-tum

Preparation time: 30 minutes
Cooking time: 20 minutes
SERVES 4

---

1 kg (2lb) dandelions

FOR GARLIC SAUCE

2 limes

3 cloves garlic

3 tbsp olive oil

a pinch cayenne

Discard the wilted leaves and wash the dandelions thoroughly.

Fill a large heavy-bottomed saucepan with 2 litres (3½ pints) salted water and bring to the boil.

Add the dandelions to the water and boil for 15-20 minutes.

Remove when cooked and drain.

Allow to cool, then squeeze out the excess moisture.

Prepare a garlic sauce with the garlic, lime and oil (see page 4).

Pour the sauce over the dandelions, mix and rub gently, using fingertips, until dandelion leaves are well coated with the sauce.

Serve warm or cold.

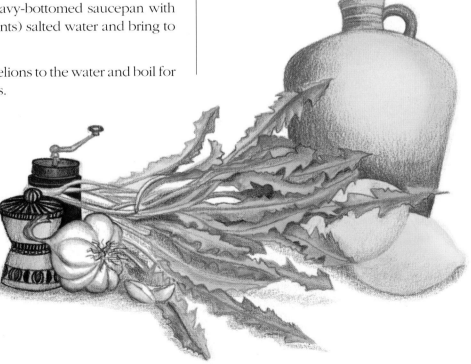

DANDELIONS WITH ONIONS

Hendbeh m'elleyeh b-basal

Preparation time: 20 minutes
Cooking time: 25 minutes
SERVES 4

1 kg (1lb) dandelions

FOR BASAL MHAMMAR

3 large onions

½ cup olive oil

pinch paprika

Prepare the dandelions following the instructions given for dandelions with garlic (page 69).

Make sure the dandelions are completely dry.

Prepare a basal mhammar with the onions and oil (see page 9).

Set aside half the fried onions on a plate.

Add the dandelions to the remaining onions.

Stir-fry over a moderate heat for 4-5 minutes.

Cover with a layer of the reserved fried onions, sprinkle with paprika and serve.

FRIED COURGETTES

Kusa me'li

Preparation time: 15 minutes
Cooking time: 20 minutes
SERVES 2

2 large courgettes

salt

½ cup ground nut oil

FOR GARLIC SAUCE

1 lemon

3 cloves garlic

4 tbsp olive oil

1 sprig fresh mint

Wash the courgettes and peel removing part of the skin, in strips (see illustration page 18). Cut into slices 1 cm (½ inch) thick.

Sprinkle with salt, leave to stand for 1 hour.

Rinse under cold water and pat dry.

In a large skillet, gently sauté the courgette slices in the ground nut oil.

Prepare a garlic sauce with the oil, garlic and the juice of one lemon (see page 4). Put the fried courgettes onto a serving dish.

Pour the garlic sauce over the courgettes and serve garnished with the mint leaves.

CHAPTER 3

GRAINS AND PULSES

BULGUR WHEAT PASTRIES WITH DRIED FRUIT
Bu emneh

Preparation time: 40 minutes
Cooking time: 10 minutes
SERVES 4

FOR THE DOUGH

1 cup very fine bulgur wheat (sraysira)
1 cup flour
1 medium onion, minced
1 tsp dried mint, crushed
salt
½ cup water

FOR THE FILLING

2 onions, thinly sliced
1 cup crushed walnuts
½ cup raisins
½ lemon
½ tsp cinnamon
a pinch cayenne
vegetable oil for frying
salt
cos lettuce for garnish

THE DOUGH

Mix together the bulgur wheat, flour, chopped onion and mint, and mix well.

Pour ½ cup of water over the mixture.

Knead well until the dough is quite smooth and leave to rest for a while.

THE FILLING

Heat 4–5 tablespoons of oil in a skillet and fry the sliced onions until they turn golden brown.

Remove fried onions and put them in a mixing bowl.

Add the crushed nuts, raisins, lemon juice, cinnamon, cayenne and salt to the onions. Mix well.

Divide the dough into small, walnut-size balls.

On a lightly floured board, flatten the balls into thin cakes about 1–2 mm (¹/₁₆ inch) thick.

Spread a tbsp of filling on half of the cakes.

Cover each of these cakes with another flat cake; press the edges together to seal them.

Heat ½ cup of oil in a skillet and fry each cake until it turns golden brown on both sides.

Serve warm or cold, garnished with cos lettuce.

74

BULGUR WHEAT WITH TOMATOES
Bulgur wheat 'a banadura

Preparation time: 15 minutes
Cooking time: 20 minutes
SERVES 4

---

3 large ripe tomatoes

1 large onion

1 cup coarse bulgur wheat

5 tbsp oil

salt, pepper

1 bunch spring onions

Skin the tomatoes, remove seeds and dice into large cubes.

Thinly slice the onion and sauté in oil until golden brown.

Add the tomatoes to the onion, mix and cook over a moderate heat for 10 minutes.

Add bulgur wheat and mix well.

Season with salt and pepper.

Add 3 cups of boiling water. Cover and bring to the boil.

Reduce heat and simmer until the water has been completely absorbed (about 20 minutes).

Serve garnished with spring onions.

LENTIL SOUP

Sorert 'adas

Preparation time: 15 minutes
Cooking time: 40 minutes
SERVES 4

1 large cup yellow lentils
½ cup short grain rice
2 medium onions
1 bunch radishes
½ cup oil
salt, pepper, cumin
toasted croûtons

Pick over and wash lentils.

Wash the rice.

Peel the onions and chop coarsely.

Heat the oil in a large heavy-bottomed saucepan and sauté the onions until they turn golden.

Add the lentils and rice to the saucepan.

Cover with 1 litre (1¾ pints) of water and bring to the boil.

Reduce to a moderate heat and continue cooking for 10 minutes.

Simmer over a low heat for another 20 minutes. Meanwhile, toast the bread to make the croûtons.

Season with salt, pepper and cumin.

Serve garnished with croûtons and radishes.

RED LENTIL SOUP

Sorert 'adas ahmar

Preparation time: 15 minutes
Cooking time: 40 minutes
SERVES 4

2 large potatoes
1 carrot
1 large onion
1 cup red lentils
½ tsp cinnamon
1 tsp cumin
salt, pepper
25 g (1oz) butter
croûtons fried in butter

Peel and dice the potatoes, carrot and onion.

Pick over the lentils and rinse in cold water.

Put lentils into large heavy-bottomed saucepan with 1 litre (1¾ pints) of water, and diced potatoes, carrot and onion.

Cover and simmer for 40 minutes.

Put the soup through a mouli-légumes or blender.

Reheat and add salt, pepper, cumin and cinnamon.

Turn off the heat and add butter. Cover, leaving the butter to melt.

Serve with the croûtons.

CHICKPEA PATTIES

Falafel

Preparation time: 30 minutes
Cooking time: 15 minutes
+ overnight soaking for fava beans and chickpeas
SERVES 6

1 cup small dried fava beans (broad beans)
1 cup chickpeas
1 tsp bicarbonate of soda
1 onion
1 bunch parsley
2 bunches coriander
1 tsp baking powder
5 cloves garlic
1 tbsp coriander seeds
1 tsp each: cumin, paprika, salt, black pepper
½ litre (just under 1 pint) peanut oil for frying
1 tomato

Pick over, wash and soak fava beans and chickpeas in water with bicarbonate of soda for 24 hours.

Purée both fava beans and chickpeas in a blender or food mill.

Wash the onion, parsley and coriander, pat dry and finely chop.

Pour over the beans and chickpeas.

Coarsely grind the coriander seeds and garlic.

Add ground garlic and coriander, spices, salt, baking powder and a few drops of water to the bean and chickpea mixture.

Knead this mixture for a few minutes.

Cover with a cloth and leave to stand for a couple of hours.

Form the mixture into walnut-size balls.

Heat ½ litre (¾ pint) of peanut oil in a suitable pan and lower the balls of mixture into the sizzling hot oil, one by one.

As they turn golden brown, remove from oil and put onto a serving dish.

Serve garnished with thin slices of tomatoes.

May also be served with sesame cream (see page 6) mixed with a little ground garlic and chopped parsley.

RED BEAN STEW

Fasulya b-zeit

Preparation time: 25 minutes
Cooking time: 1 hour
+ overnight soaking for beans
SERVES 4

Pour 1½ litres (3 pints) of salted water into a pressure-cooker.

Add the beans, peeled and diced potatoes, peeled garlic, tomato paste and bicarbonate of soda.

Seal the pressure-cooker, bring to pressure, and cook for 40 minutes.

Meanwhile, prepare a te'leyeh with the oil and onions (see page 8).

Reduce pressure, open the pressure-cooker and add the te'leyeh.

Cook for another 10 minutes (not under pressure).

Salt to taste and add a pinch of pepper.

Serve with spring onions.

The stew should remain liquid.

1 large cup of dried red beans
1 potato
1 small can of tomato paste
1 clove garlic
½ tsp bicarbonate of soda
1 large onion
½ cup oil
salt and pepper
1 bunch spring onions

Pick over the beans and soak in water overnight.

The following day, drain the soaked beans and wash again.

MONK'S KEBBEH

Kebbet rahib

Preparation time: 40 minutes
Cooking time: 45 minutes
SERVES 4

1 cup yellow lentils
1 medium head garlic
5 limes
1/2 cup olive oil
salt
FOR THE KEBBEH
1/2 cup flour
1/8 cup fine bulgur wheat
1 onion
1/2 tsp each: cinnamon, paprika
salt

Pick over and wash the lentils.

Boil 2 litres (3½ pints) of water in a large heavy-bottomed saucepan then cook the lentils for 30 minutes.

In a salad bowl mix the flour, bulgur wheat, finely chopped onions, spices and salt.

Add cup of water, and knead the mixture for a few minutes.

Shape the mixture into small walnut-sized balls and roll them in the palms of your hands.*

Place the balls on a plate sprinkled with flour.

When the lentils are cooked, add the balls and cook for another 15–20 minutes.

Prepare a garlic sauce with the lemon, garlic and oil (see page 4).

Before serving, pour the garlic sauce into the saucepan and mix.

Add the remainder of the oil and serve hot.

The stew should remain liquid.

* If the balls crumble while rolling, add a little extra flour to the mixture and knead for another few minutes.

CHICKPEA AND BEAN STEW

Makluta

Preparation time: 20 minutes
Cooking time: 1 hour 15 minutes
SERVES 4

¹/₂ cup chickpeas
¹/₄ cup dried red beans
bicarbonate of soda
¹/₂ cup cracked wheat
¹/₄ cup short grain rice
¹/₂ cup lentils
2 large onions
¹/₂ cup olive oil
salt
1 bunch radishes

Pick over the pulses and grains.

Soak the chickpeas overnight in 1 litre (1¹/₄ pints) of water into which a pinch of bicarbonate of soda has been added.

Use the same method for soaking the beans.

The following day, wash the chickpeas and beans again.

Fill a pressure-cooker with 2¹/₂ litres (4¹/₂ pints) of salted water, add the chickpeas, wheat and ¹/₂ teaspoon of bicarbonate of soda.

Cook under pressure for 40 minutes.

Reduce pressure, open the pressure-cooker and add the beans. Cook for another 20 minutes.

Open the cooker and add the rice and lentils. Close and cook for another 15 minutes.

Meanwhile, prepare the te'leyeh (see page 8).

Add the te'leyeh and salt to the pressure-cooker.

Cover and continue cooking for 5–10 minutes. (The stew should remain liquid).

Serve with radishes.

CHICKPEA AND SESAME CREAM
Hommos b'-thineh

Preparation time: 20 minutes
Cooking time: 1 hour 30 minutes
+ overnight soaking for chickpeas
SERVES 6

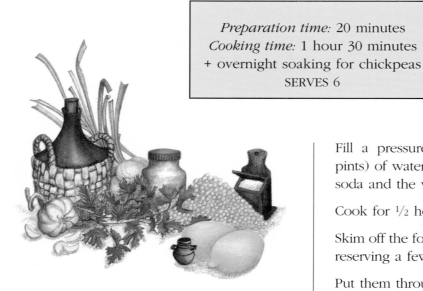

1½ cups dried chickpeas
1 tsp bicarbonate of soda
2 tbsp sesame cream
4 medium cloves garlic
juice of 2 lemons
½ tsp paprika
2 sprigs parsley
1 tbsp olive oil
1 bunch spring onions

Soak chickpeas in cold water overnight.

The next day, drain the soaked chickpeas and wash in cold water.

Fill a pressure-cooker with 2 litres (3½ pints) of water, a teaspoon bicarbonate of soda and the washed chickpeas.

Cook for ½ hour.

Skim off the foam and drain the chickpeas, reserving a few drops of the water.

Put them through a blender.

Meanwhile, prepare the sesame cream (see page 6).

Finely grind the garlic.

Mix together the chickpeas, sesame cream, garlic and lemon juice.

Beat the mixture with a fork and add a few drops of the hot water that the chickpeas were cooked in, and continue beating.

When the mixture reaches the consistency of light cream, spread it onto a serving dish.

Sprinkle with paprika, garnish with chopped parsley and a few chickpeas.

Sprinkle a few drops of oil over the surface and serve with spring onions.

SAVOURY BREAD

Man'us b-za'tar

Preparation time: 25 minutes
Cooking time: 15 minutes
SERVES 4

---

300 g (³/₄ lb) bread dough (see page 66)

---

¹/₂ cup flour

---

100 g (4oz) za'atar halabi*

---

³/₄ cup olive oil

Shape the bread dough into small walnut-sized balls.

Sprinkle with flour to prevent dough from sticking, androll out, shaping into small flat cakes, ¹/₂ cm (¹/₄ inch) thick.

Pre-heat a hot oven.

Spread a teaspoon of the za'atar mixture onto each flat cake.

Prick each one with a fork to keep dough from rising when baking.

Place in a hot oven and bake until golden.

Remove from the oven when they turn golden.

Serve hot. This dish can be served with fresh cloves of garlic, according to taste.

*Za'atar halabi is a mixtgure of thyme, sesame seeds, sumac, pistachio and cashew nuts, and can be found in oriental foodstores.

MJADRA WITH LENTILS
Mjadra b-a'das

Preparation time: 20 minutes
Cooking time: 50 minutes
SERVES 4

---
1 cup lentils
---
salt

½ cup oil
---
2 large onions
---
1 cup coarse bulgur wheat
---
1 bunch radishes
---
1 bunch spring onions

Pick over and wash lentils.

Fill a large heavy-bottomed saucepan with 2 litres (3½ pints) of water, add lentils and salt, and cook over moderate heat for ½ hour.

Meanwhile prepare te'leyeh (see page 8), with the oil and onions.

When lentils are cooked, add te'leyeh.

Boil for a few seconds.

Mix in the bulgur wheat.

Cover and boil again for 3–5 minutes.

Reduce heat and cook for another 10 minutes.

Simmer over a low heat until the water has been absorbed (5–10 minutes).

Serve garnished with radishes and small spring onions.

MJADRA WITH CHICKPEAS
Mjadra b-hommos

Preparation time: 20 minutes
Cooking time: 1 hour
+ overnight soaking for the chickpeas
SERVES 4

1 cup chickpeas
1/2 tsp bicarbonate of soda
1/2 cup oil
3 large onions
salt
1 cup coarse bulgur wheat
1 bunch spring onions

Pick over chickpeas and soak overnight in water.

The following day, drain the soaked chickpeas and wash again.

Put the chickpeas in a pressure cooker, add 1/2 teaspoon of bicarbonate of soda and 2 1/2 litres (4 1/2 pints) of water. Cook under pressure for 15 minutes.

Meanwhile, prepare te'leyeh with the oil and onions (see page 8).

Taste to check the chickpeas are cooked.

When chickpeas are cooked, stir in the te'leyeh and add salt.

Mix in the bulgur wheat and follow the instructions for preparing mjadra with lentils, opposite.

Serve garnished with spring onions.

MJADRA WITH RED KIDNEY BEANS
Mjadra b-lubyeh

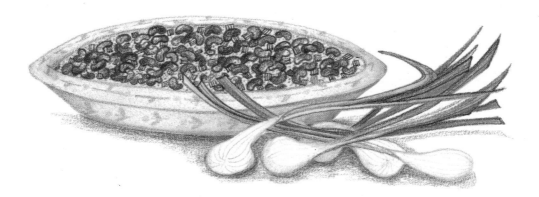

Preparation time: 20 minutes
Cooking time: 50 minutes
+ overnight soaking for beans
SERVES 4

1 large cup red kidney beans
salt
3 large onions
½ cup olive oil
1 large cup coarse bulgur wheat
1 bunch spring onions

Pick over the beans and soak overnight.

Wash the soaked beans thoroughly and put into a pressure cooker with 2 litres (3½ pints) water. Add salt.

Seal cooker and cook under pressure for 30 minutes.

Meanwhile, prepare the te'leyeh (see page 8) with the onions and oil.

When the beans are done, mix in both the te'leyeh and the bulgur wheat.

Cover and boil for 5 minutes, then reduce to a moderate heat and cook for a further 5 minutes.

Finally, simmer over a low heat for 10 minutes until water has been completely absorbed.

Serve either with spring onions or a tomato and onion salad (see page 34).

LENTIL PURÉE

Mseffeyeh

Preparation time: 20 minutes
Cooking time: 45 minutes
SERVES 4

1¹⁄₂ cups yellow lentils
¹⁄₂ cup short grain rice
3 medium onions
¹⁄₂ cup peanut oil
salt
1 bunch radishes

Pick over the lentils and wash both the lentils and the rice.

Pour both into a large heavy-bottomed saucepan with 2¹⁄₂ litres (4¹⁄₂ pints) salted water.

Cook covered for 45 minutes.

Meanwhile, prepare a basal mhammar with the oil and onions (see page 9).

Set aside half of the basal mhammar on a plate. This will be used for garnishing.

When rice and lentils are cooked, strain and reserve the stock.

Put rice and lentils through a blender.

Return the puréed mixture to the stock and reheat.

Add the other half of the basal mhammar with the oil used for frying.

Boil for a couple of minutes until the mixture thickens.

Season to taste.

Serve garnished with the remainder of the fried onions and the radishes.

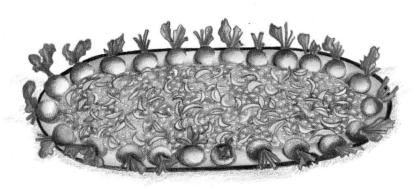

RESTA WITH LENTILS

Resta b-adas

Preparation time: 1 hour
Cooking time: 45 minutes
SERVES 4

| 1 cup yellow lentils |
| 3 large onions |
| ½ cup olive oil |
| salt |
| 2 bunches coriander |

FOR THE DOUGH

| 150 g (6oz) flour |
| a pinch of salt |
| 1 tbsp water |

Pick over lentils and wash thoroughly.

Put lentils in a large heavy-bottomed saucepan, fill with 2½ litres (4½ pints) water, and cook for ½ hour.

Meanwhile, prepare dough with the flour, salt and water. Knead for 10 minutes until the dough is smooth and soft.

Roll out the dough as thinly as you possibly can.

Sprinkle the surface of the dough with flour and cut into strips 2.5 cm (1 inch) wide. Then cut, crosswise, into small pieces (see drawing).

Prepare basal mhammar with oil and onions (see page 9).

When lentils are cooked, add the strips of dough, half of the basal mhammar and all the oil in which the onions were fried.

Add salt and cook for another 15 minutes.

Wash coriander, chop coarsely and stir-fry in oil for a few minutes.

Before serving, add coriander and the rest of the onions to the lentils.

Mix and serve hot on a lightly floured serving dish.

The resta should remain liquid.

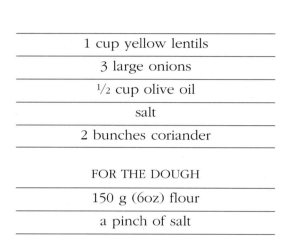

RESTA WITH RED KIDNEY BEANS

Resta b-lubyeh

Preparation time: 1 hour
Cooking time: 45 minutes
+ overnight soaking for beans
SERVES 4

1 cup red kidney beans
½ tsp bicarbonate of soda
3 large onions
½ cup olive oil
salt
FOR THE DOUGH
150 g (5oz) flour
pinch salt
1 tbsp water

Pick over the beans and soak in cold water overnight.

The following day, wash beans and put them in a large pressure cooker with 2 litres (3 pints) water.

Add ½ teaspoon bicarbonate of soda and cook under pressure for 30 minutes.

Meanwhile, prepare dough as indicated in recipe for resta with lentils, opposite.

Prepare a basal mhammar with the oil and onions (see page 9) and add it to the pressure cooker. Bring to the boil (not under pressure).

When boiling, add the strips of dough (prepared as for the resta with lentils, opposite).

Simmer for another 15 minutes (the resta should remain liquid)

Add salt and serve hot.

RICE WITH VERMICELLI
Rozz b-s'arriyyeh

Preparation time: 15 minutes
Cooking time: 25 minutes
SERVES 4

1 cup long grain rice (e.g. basmati)
30 g (1oz) butter
½ cup vermicelli
a large pinch of cinnamon
salt, pepper

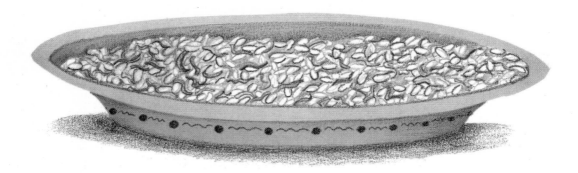

Wash and drain rice.

Melt butter in a large heavy-bottomed saucepan.

Gently sauté the vermicelli in the butter, stirring constantly until it turns golden brown.

Add the rice and continue cooking for another 5–10 minutes while stirring over a moderate heat.

Season with the salt, pepper and cinnamon.

Mix well and add 2 cups of boiling water.*

Cover and boil for 3–5 minutes.

Reduce to a moderate heat and allow the rice to swell for a couple of minutes before serving.

* The same cup should be used for all measurements.

RICE WITH GREEN FAVA BEANS

Rozz b-ful

> *Preparation time:* 30 minutes
> *Cooking time:* 40 minutes
> SERVES 4

1½ kg (3lb) green fava beans (young broad beans)
2 onions
½ cup peanut oil
1 cup rice
salt, pepper

Remove the outer shells of the fava beans.

Place in a colander, wash in cold water and leave to drain.

Peel the onions, cut into very thin slices and stir-fry in ½ cup of oil until they turn golden brown.

Add beans and continue cooking for another 5–10 minutes.

Add 1½ cups of boiling water, cover saucepan and bring to the boil.

Cook over a moderate heat until the water has completely evaporated.

Taste to check if well cooked.

Wash and drain the rice and add to the beans.

Season with salt and pepper.

Mix well and add 2 cups of boiling water, cover and bring to the boil for 10 minutes.

Reduce to a moderate heat and continue cooking until all the water is completely absorbed.

Remove from the heat and leave rice to swell for 5–10 minutes before serving.

91

RICE WITH LENTILS

'Adas 'a rozz

Preparation time: 20 minutes
Cooking time: 1 hour
SERVES 4

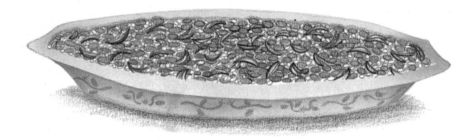

| 1 cup yellow lentils |
| salt |
| 3 medium onions |
| ½ cup oil |
| ½ cup short grain rice |

Pick over lentils and wash carefully.

Put lentils in a large heavy-bottomed saucepan filled with 2 litres (3½ pints) of water. Add salt and bring to the boil.

Reduce to a moderate heat, cover and continue cooking for ½ hour.

Meanwhile, prepare basal mhammar with the oil and onions (see page 9).

Set aside half the fried onions on a plate.

When lentils are cooked, add the other half of the onions and their frying oil.

Add the washed rice to the lentils.

Cover and boil for 5 minutes, then reduce to a moderate heat and cook for a further 10 minutes.

Finally, simmer over a low heat until done (5–10 minutes).

Garnish with the remaining fried onions and serve.

LENTILS IN LIME JUICE

'Adas b-ha'mod

Preparation time: 1 hour 20 minutes
Cooking time: 40 minutes
SERVES 4

| 1 cup yellow lentils |
| 6 small chard leaves |
| 1 large onion |
| 1 head garlic |
| 5 limes |
| 1 cup olive oil |
| salt |

Pick over lentils, wash and put in a large heavy-bottomed saucepan filled with 2 litres (3½ pints) water.

Boil for 15 minutes.

Meanwhile, wash the chard leaves, remove the ribs, and chop coarsely both the ribs and the leaves.

Cook the diced chard ribs for ¼ hour, then add ribs to the lentils.

Cook for 10 minutes.

Add the chard leaves and simmer for another 10 minutes.

Taste to check if it is cooked.

Using the garlic, oil and the juice of 3 of the limes, prepare a garlic sauce (see page 4).

Pour the sauce into the saucepan and stir.

Boil for 2–3 minutes.

Serve hot with slices of lime.

(The adas b-ha'mod should remain liquid.)

CHAPTER 4

EGGS AND DAIRY PRODUCE

AMHIYYEH WITH YOGURT
Amhiyyeh b-laban

Preparation time: 20 minutes
Cooking time: 1 hour
SERVES 4

---

1 large cup cracked wheat

1 bunch fresh mint

½ head garlic

6 pots yogurt (preferably goats' milk)

salt

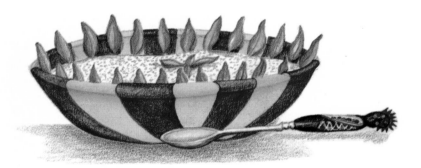

Fill a pressure-cooker with 2 litres (3½ pints) water and add salt.

Add the wheat, cover tightly and bring to the boil.

Cook for an hour from the time the pan is up to pressure.

Leave to cook and remove the lid.

Taste to check if cooked.

Wash the mint, pat dry. Set aside a few leaves to use later as garnish and crush the rest together with the garlic.

Empty the pots of yogurt into a bowl and beat with a fork.

Stir in crushed mint and garlic with the yogurt.

Pour this mixture into the pressure cooker and stir for a few minutes.

Season to taste.

Serve warm garnished with mint leaves.

The amhiyyeh must remain liquid.

MA'KRUN WITH YOGURT

Ma'krun b-laban

Preparation time: 40 minutes
Cooking time: 30 minutes
SERVES 4

FOR THE MA'KRUN DOUGH

150 g (6oz) flour

a pinch salt

1 tbsp water

¼ cup rice

salt

1 bunch fresh mint

4 cloves garlic

6 pots plain yogurt (preferably goats'
milk)

Mix the flour with the salt and water.

Knead well until the dough is smooth and
soft. Roll out the dough, using a rolling pin,
to thickness of ½ cm (¼ inch).

Sprinkle the surface with flour and cut with
a sharp knife into very thin strips.

Cut the strips into small squares.

Spread out the squares of dough onto a
lightly floured surface to prevent them from
sticking.

Fill a large heavy-bottomed saucepan with
2 litres (3½ pints) of water, add salt and
bring to the boil.

Add the washed rice and cook for about
¼ hour.

Add the squares of dough and simmer for
another ¼ hour.

Turn off the heat.

Wash mint and pat dry.

Finely crush the mint and garlic.

Mix together the crushed mint, garlic and
yogurt and beat the mixture with a fork.

When the mixture in the saucepan has
cooled, stir in the yogurt, garlic and mint
mixture.

Mix together well and serve.

The ma'krun must remain liquid.

AUBERGINES WITH YOGURT
Batinjan b-laban

Preparation time: 30 minutes
SERVES 4

| 1 large aubergine |
| salt |
| 1 tbsp sesame cream |
| 4 pots plain yogurt (preferably goats' milk) |
| ½ bunch of fresh mint |
| 1 large clove garlic |

Wash the aubergine and cut into slices 1 cm (½ inch) thick.

Sprinkle with salt and leave to stand for a good hour.

Heat oil in a large skillet and lightly brown the aubergine slices on both sides.

Cut the slices of aubergines into small cubes.

Beat together the sesame cream and yogurt with a fork.

Crush the garlic and stir into the yogurt and sesame cream.

Beat again.

Add the fried cubes of aubergines.

Mix well, season to taste and serve garnished with mint leaves.

RICE WITH YOGURT

Rozz b-laban

Preparation time: 15 minutes
Cooking time: 20 minutes
SERVES 4

½ cup short grain rice

---

1 bunch fresh mint

---

2 large cloves garlic

---

6 pots of plain yogurt (preferably
goats' milk)

½ cup pine nuts

---

salt

Wash rice and cook in a large heavy-bottomed saucepan filled with 1½ litres (2¾ pints) water.

Wash mint and pat dry.

When rice is cooked, remove and leave to cool.

Meanwhile, wash the garlic and mint. Set aside some mint leaves to use later as garnish.

Mix together the ground garlic, mint and yogurt.

Beat the mixture until it is smooth and creamy.

Add to the mixture the cooked (and still warm) rice.

Add salt and mix well.

Serve in a soup tureen, sprinkled with fried pine nuts and garnished with mint leaves.

CUCUMBER WITH YOGURT

Kyar b-laban

Preparation time: 20 minutes
+ 2 hours standing time for cucumbers
SERVES 4

1 cucumber
salt
4 pots plain yogurt (preferably goats' milk)
juice of ½ lemon
½ bunch fresh mint
a pinch cayenne
1 clove garlic

Peel and slice cucumbers.

Sprinkle with salt and leave to stand for 2 hours.

Rinse the slices of cucumbers in cold water and pat dry.

In a salad bowl, beat the yogurt with the juice of half a lemon using a fork.

Wash the mint and pat dry. Set aside some leaves to use as garnish.

Crush the garlic and mint.

Add the crushed garlic and mint to the yogurt and mix well.

Mix in the slices of cucumber.

Sprinkle with cayenne and garnish with mint leaves.

EGGS WITH TOMATOES

Beyd a banadura

> *Preparation time:* 10 minutes
> *Cooking time:* 5 minutes
> SERVES 1

1 ripe tomato
1 tbsp olive oil
2 eggs
a dash each: cinnamon, pepper, cumin
salt
50 g (2oz) black olives

Wash the tomato, peel, cut in half and remove the seeds.

Heat oil in a skillet until it sizzles.

Break the eggs into the pan.

With your fingertips, press the tomato halves over the eggs.

Season with salt, pepper, cinnamon and cumin and cook for about 3 minutes.

Serve garnished with black olives.

EGGS IN OLIVE OIL

Beyd me'li b-zeit

Preparation time: 2 minutes
Cooking time: 3–5 minutes
SERVES 1

3 tbsp olive oil

2 eggs

salt

½ bunch fresh mint

1 bunch spring onions

Heat the olive oil in skillet until it sizzles, then reduce heat and break the eggs into the pan.

Sprinkle with salt and fry over a high heat.

Spoon some of the hot oil over the eggs.

Repeat until a white layer forms over the surface of the eggs and covers the yolks.

Remove and serve on a plate garnished with mint leaves and spring onions.

EGGS FRIED WITH GREEN GARLIC LEAVES

Beyd b-wara'tum

Preparation time: 10 minutes
Cooking time: 15 minutes
SERVES 2

1 bunch green garlic leaves (if not available, leek or chives can be substituted)
2 tbsp olive oil
2 eggs
salt, pepper

Wash the garlic leaves, pat dry and cut into ½ cm (¼ inch) pieces.

Heat the olive oil in a skillet, add the cut garlic leaves and stir-fry until light brown.

Break the eggs over the garlic leaves, and season to taste with salt and pepper.

Mix, allow to firm, and serve hot.

EGG PANCAKES WITH PARSLEY
Ojjeh b-ba'dunes

Preparation time: 25 minutes
Cooking time: 3–5 minutes per pancake
SERVES 6

½ bunch fresh mint

1 bunch parsley

2 shallots

salt, pepper, cinnamon

4 eggs

ground nut oil

1 tomato

1 lettuce

Wash and finely chop the parsley and mint.

Mince the shallots and mix well with a pinch of salt.

Mix together parsley, mint and shallots and season with the spices.

Break in the eggs and beat with a fork.

Heat half a cup of oil in a large frying pan.

Once the oil is sizzling, pour a tablespoon of the mixture into the pan and spread out evenly with a fork or spatula, to form a pancake.

Fry both sides of the pancake until golden brown.

Remove from the skillet and drain on a paper towel.

Serve pancakes on a bed of crispy lettuce and garnish with slices of tomato.

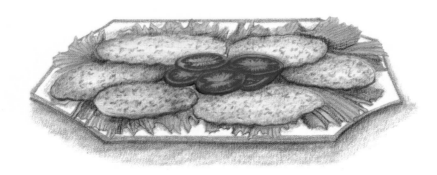

FRIED EGGS WITH TOMATOES AND ONIONS

Mfarkeh

Preparation time: 15 minutes
Cooking time: 25 minutes
SERVES 2

2 ripe tomatoes, peeled and de-seeded

1 large onion, chopped

4 tbsp olive oil

salt, pepper

4 eggs

a pinch of cumin

Chop the tomatoes coarsely.

Heat oil in a skillet and fry the chopped onions until they turn golden brown.

Mix the tomatoes with the onions in the skillet and stir-fry the mixture for 15–20 minutes over a low heat.

Season to taste with salt and pepper.

Break the eggs over tomatoes and onions.

Cook until egg whites are firm, keeping the yolks whole.

Sprinkle with cumin and serve hot.

CHEESE FILO

Ftayer b-jeben

Preparation time: 20 minutes
Cooking time: 3–5 minutes per unit
SERVES 6

| 500 g (1lb) of a'khawi cheese* |
| ½ bunch parsley |
| 1 tbsp creme fraiche or double cream |
| a pinch nutmeg |
| salt, pepper |
| 1 roll of filo |
| ground nut oil for frying |
| 1 head lettuce |

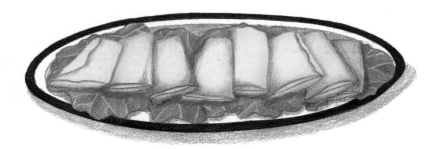

Mash the cheese with a fork.

Wash parsley, pat dry and chop finely.

Mix together the mashed cheese, chopped parsley, cream, nutmeg, salt and pepper.

Cut the layers of filo into 15 cm x 10 cm (6 x 4 inch) rectangles.

Put a tablespoon of filling on each rectangle.

Fold the sides over the filling and roll.

Fry in sizzling hot oil.

Serve hot on a bed of crispy lettuce..

* A'khawi cheese is sold in oriental food stores but if not available an Italian cheese like mozzarella or ricotta can be substituted.

EGG ROLLS WITH YOGURT
'Ojjeh b-laban

Preparation time: 15 minutes
Cooking time: 5–7 minutes per roll
+ overnight draining for yogurt
SERVES 4

4 pots plain yogurt (preferably goats' milk)
1 bunch parsley
½ bunch fresh mint
1 onion
4 eggs
50 g (2oz) pine nuts
a pinch each: cinnamon, pepper
salt
½ cup vegetable oil
2 tomatoes

Place a dampened cloth in a large colander and pour the yogurt into it.

Fold the edges of the cloth over the yogurt and leave to drain during the night.

The following day, empty the drained yogurt into a bowl.

Wash and finely chop the parsley and mint.

Mince the onion.

Beat the eggs in a bowl with a fork.

Add the parsley, mint, onion, flour and spices to the eggs.

Add salt and mix well.

Heat half a cup of oil in a skillet.

Pour in 2 tablespoons of the egg mixture and evenly spread to form a pancake.

Spread a tablespoon of the drained yogurt onto the pancake and roll up the pancake over the yogurt using a knife and fork.

Fry both sides for another 3 minutes.

Use up all the mixture in this way.

Place the rolls in a serving dish, sprinkle with pine nuts.

Serve warm, with sliced tomatoes.

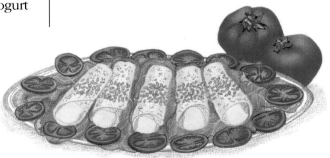

EGG PANCAKES WITH COURGETTES

'Ojjet kusa

Preparation time: 15 minutes
Cooking time: 3–6 minutes per pancake
SERVES 4

2 small courgettes
1 sprig parsley
4 shallots
1 tbsp flour
a pinch cinnamon
salt, pepper
4 eggs
ground nut oil for frying

Add the finely chopped parsley, minced shallots, flour, cinnamon, pepper and salt.

Mix together and break the eggs over the mixture.

Beat this mixture for a couple of minutes.

Heat oil in a frying pan and pour in two tablespoons of the mixture.

Spread evenly into a small pancake, using a spatula.

Fry on both sides until golden brown.

Remove the pancake from the pan and put onto a warm serving dish.

Use up all the mixture in this way.

Serve warm.

Peel and dice the courgettes and boil in salted water.

When cooked, place in a colander and rinse under cold water.

Squeeze to remove all excess moisture.

Spread out the courgettes on a paper towel to draw off any water, then place in a bowl.